Stories from the Garden Shed

Stories from the Garden Shed

Merrill Williams

Weeping Willow Books

Stories from the Garden Shed
©2021 Merrill Williams

All rights reserved. No part of this book may be used or reproduced in any manner whatsoever without written permission.

ISBN 9781732970670

Published by
Weeping Willow Books
Santa Fe NM
www.weepingwillowbooks.com
info@weepingwillowbooks.com

Design by Don Mitchell

Dedication

This book is dedicated to my children,
my grandchildren, and
my unborn great-grandchildren.
This is their story, too.

And to my dear brother, Jamie,
who left us before this book was finished.

Contents

Prologue	9
A Life Ends	15
A Search Begins	19
Uncovering Mom's Past	23
The Past Comes to Life	26
My Merrill Namesake	31
Franklin Merrill and Rebecca Jane Raplee	42
Joseph Speakman and Phoebe Anderton	47
Glendon Clyde Speakman and Golda Alice Hall	60
My Parents, James Russell Tippett and Glenda Alice Speakman	70
Eva Jane Tippett	81
George William Tippett	92
George Henry Tippett and Corinda Lee Morrish	105
William Morrish and Catherine Lydia Williams	121
Isaac Williams and Catherine Ley	129
William Tippett and Elizabeth Jane Pentecost	140
William Tippett and Sarah Rogers	153

WHAT'S IN A NAME?	162
WHO CARES ABOUT ANCESTORS?	165
ACKNOWLEDGEMENTS	169
MERRILL WILLIAMS FAMILY TREE	171
MAP OF CORNWALL	172

Prologue

My father died when I was fifty years old, taking with him the last link I had to my paternal ancestors. Then, when my mother passed away seventeen years later, the sense of loss I experienced was outweighed by the overwhelming feeling of having been pushed along the continuum of life to take up a new role. As the eldest of my siblings, I had suddenly become the matriarch of the family, the archetypal wise old woman who was to keep the stories alive for the generations that followed. It was not a role I was prepared to fulfill.

As executor of my mother's estate, it fell to me to handle the "important" papers — the tax returns, the trust documents, and the bank accounts — but equally important, and infinitely more fun, were the boxes of personal mementos. As my siblings and I sorted through old scrapbooks, we came upon a collection of old photos that would take my life in a new direction: reconstructing our ancestry.

The sheer volume of photos and clippings was overwhelming. I couldn't even imagine where to start to make sense of it all. My limited experience with online family history sites with their vast wells of genealogical records guaranteed that I would soon find names and dates, but I wanted more. I wanted to know the story of these individuals, who they were, where they lived, and what they did. I wanted to "meet" these people, not just hang their name tags on a tree. And deep down, I hoped that by knowing them, I'd start to know a little more about how I came to be me.

It became obvious to me that, to be really meaningful, my research needed to focus on what I could find in records that were still available. How far back would I have to go?

Some simple arithmetic provided an answer. Because the number of direct ancestors doubles every generation, by the time I worked my way back, say, ten generations (if that were even feasible), my cast of characters would number more than a thousand! That would be completely out of the question, so I adjusted my expectations and re-defined my task: to find out what I could about the three or four generations that preceded me. So I re-calculated: If I were to start with my two parents, my four grandparents, and my eight great-grandparents, and end with my sixteen great-great-grandparents, my family history would comprise the life stories of thirty individuals, a more manageable task.

For this book, I elected to follow my direct ancestors (no siblings, no cousins) back four generations. Once I got into it, though, I did take a couple of side jaunts to explore my father's siblings because I just couldn't resist. In the end, as many genealogists know, the stories that get told are the stories for which information is available. Some branches of my family tree extend back to the early 1600s; others are much shorter and dead-end abruptly. Records are lost, names are misspelled, people with the same name get confused and soon the story no longer makes sense and disappears forever.

What I knew about either side of my family before starting this book was scant. My mother had told me I was named after my grandmother's mother, Mary Ann Merrill, repurposing her last name for my first name. I had a vague memory of other last names she would also rattle off: Speakman, Hall, Raplee, Wagoner, Anderton. They all seemed to hail from the Midwestern states of Illinois, Kansas, Iowa and Oklahoma. No one mentioned an immigrant ancestor, so I had always considered my mother's ancestors as "the Americans," an appallingly ignorant notion held by those who forget that unless their ancestry is Native American, all Americans are descended from immigrants to this country. My research would soon show that while one side of my maternal bloodline had been early settlers in New England (and several had shed that blood in the American Revolution fighting against their British king), the most recent maternal ancestor to immigrate from England was my great-grandfather, John Speakman, who arrived from Lancashire in 1868, thus confirming my very British DNA.

On my father's side, I was told the most recent English immigrant was my grandfather, George Henry Tippett, who arrived in 1879. He died eighteen years before I was born, so my knowledge of him was reduced to what little my father had said about him: he was a miner from Redruth in Cornwall who came to California to work in the gold mines. For many American children, the mystique of the Gold Rush and the history of late nineteenth-century mining is fascinating and I was enthralled with the story I invented for this grandfather I never knew. Although it didn't take long before I learned the real story and had to let go of some of those myths; any person who takes the risk of leaving family behind to venture to a new land, as he did, is a hero in the eyes of the generations that follow.

As I was to find out much later, my grandfather was not the most recent immigrant at all. It was my great-grandfather William Morrish who arrived some fifteen years earlier in 1862. Even as a child, I could see my dad knew almost nothing at all about his Morrish ancestors, so this miscalculation was understandable. I wish he were still alive so I could share with him what I learned about his incorrigible grandfather, William Morrish.

The unsung heroes in many family stories are the women. Because they have traditionally been treated as peripheral throughout history, there are far, far fewer records available to document their lives. Until relatively recently, women did not own property, did not vote, did not hold office, and did not run businesses. Their roles were limited to daughter, wife, mother and widow – and always linked to a man. I was horrified to discover that when my immigrant male ancestors applied for U.S. citizenship, their wives took no such action. Because they were considered a mere appendage of their husbands, once their spouses became citizens so did they; the women were swept into their new status by default, not through any legal action taken in their own names. Of course, we can guess what the women were doing in those early days: they cooked and fetched water, fed the family and maintained the home, planted and harvested the garden, stitched their clothing and countless other tasks that we in the twenty-first century can't even imagine.

Not to be forgotten is that these women gave birth to as many as a dozen babies – without the aid of modern medicine – and still continued their hard work. Way too many of my female ancestors died very young, like my great-great-grandmother Rebecca Jane Raplee Merrill, who died one week after giving birth to her ninth child at the age of thirty-nine. As one final injustice, her headstone in the Missouri graveyard where she was buried has been knocked over and all that remains is a heap of crumbling stone. Happily, the plight of women changed dramatically in the twentieth and twenty-first centuries, and the stories of some of my more recent female ancestors provide clear testament to those changes.

Because I am not a trained genealogist and do not have a librarian's research skills, I am sure I have not exhausted all the resources that are available. Surely there are newspapers, vital records and photos that have never been digitized and put online that remain hidden in vaults or trunks, or boxes in someone else's garden shed, somewhere out there. As an amateur family historian, I make no claims that my work has been flawless. Certainly, there are errors and omissions in this book, and for that I accept full responsibility. My intent was to provide my family with a good – if not perfect – description of where they came from, something they could pass on to their children and grandchildren. Perhaps this book will one day be found in an old box in a garden shed by a great-grandchild who will become the family's next historian. And there will be so much more to tell, because a family's story is never finished.

A Life Ends

So it was settled. "Okay, I'll see you tomorrow afternoon," I cheerfully told my son after we'd agreed on plans for me to pay a long-overdue visit to his family, who live up the coast of California. I was eager to see my two young grandchildren, and weekends for this family of two students and two educators were the only free days when visits were possible.

My house in Ojai was secured and readied to be vacant for a few days, mail delivery was on hold, my suitcase was packed, and the only undone chore was a last-minute visit to my ninety-two-year-old mother, who lived in a local nursing home. I had intended to drop by to see her at the dinner hour but, exhausted, I talked myself into turning it into a morning visit on my way out of town instead. She'll be fresher and more alert, I told myself. I'll take her picture and share it with the grandkids when I arrive, I decided. And with that I fell into bed.

A few minutes past midnight, I was jarred awake by the angry ringing of my cell phone. Even in the murky awareness of half-sleep, I sensed something was very wrong. An unfamiliar voice identified herself as a caretaker at my mother's nursing home.

"I'm very sorry," she said, "but your mom passed away a few minutes ago."

I leapt out of bed, threw on whatever clothes were draped over a chair and jumped into my car. The streets in town, blanketed with a chilly spring fog that muted all sound, were deserted. I could only hear my own heart beating loudly in my chest. I kept blinking my eyes, trying to focus on the reality of what had happened.

I was met by the owner of the nursing home, who gave me a hug and shared her condolences. I couldn't come up with a response and only asked who had been with my mother when she passed. I was relieved when we were joined by Chang, my mother's favorite caretaker.

Chang, a young Chinese woman from the Philippines who spoke little English, had developed a very close relationship with my mother and rarely left her side. Chang fed her, bathed her, and sang to her. With my mom's end-stage dementia and Chang's heavily accented English, I doubt their "conversations" were much more than the chipper banter between a doting mother and a helpless baby. But the love between them was very real.

Chang led me into my mother's room and invited me to sit down where she herself had spent the last few hours. In broken sentences, Chang described how my mother's breathing had become more and more intermittent, and that during the gaps between breaths, Chang had prayed out loud, "Don't leave me; I'm not ready!"

Another breath followed by a longer silence. "No! You can't die, not until the cold wind blows!"

Perplexed, I stared at Chang, looking for an explanation. Chang explained that in her culture, when a person dies, her spirit can be felt as it passes from the body. "I told your mom that I would wait to feel the wind before I could believe she was really gone."

Stunned, I sank into the bedside chair and asked to be left alone with my mother. I remained there, alone, for at least an hour, maybe two, until I pulled out my cell phone. I wanted to remember everything Chang had told me so I could share the story with my family. As I typed notes into my phone, I was suddenly aware of an eerie sensation: the hairs on the back of my neck were prickling and I felt cold air on my shoulders. Terrified, I turned around abruptly and saw that the window had been left barely open. A perfectly logical explanation, or had Chang been right all along? My mother's spirit was leaving, and I knew this night had changed more than just a weekend; it had changed my life.

Back home, I sat in my kitchen sipping hot tea and waited for the dawn. I gazed out at the fog that seemed to have seeped inside the house to envelop me in a chilly embrace. I listened for the sounds of creatures beginning to stir, but there was only silence, a heavy, thick silence.

When the first light finally arrived, I had gathered my thoughts enough to know what had to be done next. There were children and grandchildren and siblings to call, and each one would have questions, lots of questions. I needed to be able to tell the story of this night.

I did not know it then, but I had more questions than anybody.

A Search Begins

My head throbbed as a maelstrom of tasks swirled around in my exhausted brain. I spent the rest of the day in and out of bed, trying to regain enough energy to tackle the laundry list of to-dos, and adding more and more tasks to the list.

My head finally cleared the next day. After coordinating a date with the church for a service with the various arrival times of family members scattered all over the country, I set about making dozens of phone calls and writing emails to Mom's friends. I followed up with the nursing home and the hospice team. I cleared my work calendar. I booked hotel rooms and researched airport transportation for the out-of-towners.

Retreating to my office a few hours later, I dug into my files and located my mom's pre-need instructions. A few years back, my mother had handed me a red file folder containing her contract with a local funeral home. With a sigh of relief, I silently thanked her for taking at least a few chores off my plate. No cold-calling the funeral home to set up a preliminary meeting and starting from scratch. Not only had she prepaid her burial and funeral costs, but in the contract section entitled "Last Wishes" she had carefully called out the music for her service. A few of the hymns she'd chosen I knew well, but there were a couple that were entirely unknown to me. I spent a few hours on the computer researching lyrics to these old classics, listening to audio clips and printing out the sheet music to give to the church's organist in case she too was as much in the dark as I was.

But "Last Wishes" didn't end there. Mom also described what clothing she wanted to be buried in. I knew nothing in her closet would fit her, given her dramatic weight loss over the past year, so I suddenly had a shopping trip to make: gray suit, pink blouse and pearl earrings. I couldn't believe it. Who plans their fashion statement for their own wake? I called my sister, Susan, in Vermont, who calmed me down by assuring me, "We'll deal with it when I get there."

A few days later, Susan arrived and we had a game plan. Being pragmatists, we agreed that since the requested outfit would see only very short-term use, we'd purchase something that granted Mom's wishes but was inexpensive. We headed to JC Penney's, known for its extensive petite department, and it didn't take long before we'd found a small blouse, extra-small gray suit, and a pair of faux pearl earrings. Perfect.

At the counter, Susan and I arranged our purchases for the sales clerk and shared a satisfied smile. The woman behind the counter was a cheerful soul who set about admiring each item.

"Such a lovely outfit," she chirped. "Is it for a special occasion?" Susan and I blinked in shock, and as I murmured, "Yes, it is," she and I abruptly turned around to stifle the guffaws about to explode from our mouths.

There was only one task left that I had already started: writing my mother's eulogy. In the long wait leading up to this moment – her declining physical and mental health, the ever-more frequent calls to and from the hospice nurse and the nursing home – I had a lot of time to contemplate my mother's long life. One day I just sat down and started writing.

On the day I delivered the eulogy in the church, I knew that focusing on Mom's musical career was how her local friends knew her best. In Ojai, she had formed a women's choral group that enjoyed success performing at various small venues. But that was just a small slice of her life. Very few in the church knew anything about her previous seven decades when she lived in New York, where not only did she have a long musical career but a long history of community leadership. Mom had been the daughter who left her Midwestern roots to marry a publishing executive and raise a family in New York. I knew precious little about her life in Kansas City, even less about her parents and grandparents. Indeed, most of Mom's ancestors were total strangers to me.

Over the next several days, as the family gathered for the funeral, my grandchildren peppered me with questions about their great-grandmother. My brother reminded me that I had once upon a time started a family tree that stopped just a few branches up the trunk before I hit dead ends in every direction. The names I had added to that early tree came from hearing them mentioned occasionally in fleeting conversations with my parents.

I had stopped trying to build a family tree when it became obvious it was going to require a lot more work and research. And at that moment, I was too overwhelmed to even consider re-launching a project of such magnitude. My job was to focus on paperwork, dealing with Mom's accountant and lawyer, and performing my duty as her executor. I was now head of the family.

Uncovering Mom's Past

Being the executor of an estate is a God-awful job. It requires nerves of steel, the patience of a saint, and the ability to set aside every other part of your life to take on mountains of paperwork and sort through boxes of documents and tax returns. I had none of these attributes and soon became short-tempered and irritable.

My mother's friends would comment on what a lovely home she had, what beautiful artifacts and furniture she had. And wasn't I lucky she had left such beautiful things to her children? But after a few weeks of poking around in shelves, closets, cupboards and bookcases, I couldn't see beauty; I could only see stuff, tons of stuff, that needed to be discarded.

I summoned the family and announced that we needed to have a giant garage sale, and that if there was anything they wanted for themselves, now was the time to claim it. So one spring weekend, I walked every room and hallway with my kids and siblings to consider the disposition of hundreds of household items: china, crystal, silverware, artwork, beds and bedding, appliances, tables and chairs, books, and more than a few Victorian loveseats.

Susan and I climbed into the attic and found an old cardboard box with Mom's wedding gown that had been rolled tightly into a bulky wad where it had remained for almost seventy years, something we'd never seen before. We unfurled yards of pale pink voile that started to resemble the framed wedding portrait that hung in her bedroom. For a few hopeful moments, we each had thoughts of saving it for some future bride, but right before our eyes, the fragile voile started to crumble and our dreams disintegrated. With teary eyes, we added that sweet wedding gown to the trash barrel. I ran to grab Mom's wedding portrait off the wall, knowing the black-and-white photograph would now be our only glimpse of how she looked on her wedding day in 1940.

To my surprise and delight, several large pieces of furniture found new homes in Santa Cruz and San Ramon where my son and brother lived. Even with so much claimed by the family, there remained a ton of stuff to deal with. I shipped a number of pieces of delicate crystal to my son in Boston. I contacted a local antiques dealer to discuss a consignment sale, plus a few of Mom's close friends who might want a souvenir of their friendship with her, and still there was just so much stuff.

On the day of the garage sale, I reminded Jamie and Susan that we needed to try to overlook sentimental feelings and focus on the goal: to get rid of as much as we could, even if the price was insultingly low. At the end of that exhausting day, very little of what was left meant much to the family. I felt we'd done a respectable job of emptying out her house in preparation for listing it for sale. I engaged a longtime friend, the same Realtor who had sold the house to my parents some twenty-five years before, and after a few weeks the property was sold. There was not much joy in that transaction, only sadness that the last physical manifestation of my mother and father's presence on this earth was no longer ours. What we had left were the boxes of photographs and postcards we'd found in the garden shed.

The Past Comes to Life

A few months after my mother's death, after I'd taken care of the lion's share of estate work and the closing up of her house and belongings, Jamie and I, along with his wife, Erika, agreed to meet once again to dive into the contents of the last boxes in our parents' garden shed.

Thank goodness Erika had cleaned up the boxes. Gone were the cobwebs and the caked-on dust. As we carefully lifted the lids, we couldn't help but marvel that these old photographs had somehow survived years in a metal shed alongside garden fertilizers and pesticides, old tools crusted with dirt, discarded seed packets, and a lawnmower that reeked of engine oil. It looked as if these ancient photos were still tucked into their original albums, untouched for decades. We grinned in anticipation of the treasures that awaited us.

Erika is a natural curator and had carefully sorted through some of the old photos to put them into some semblance of order. Two large heaps awaited our perusal: photos from our dad's family, the Tippetts, and others from our mom's family, the Speakmans. I gravitated first to the Speakman pile and carefully lifted out of an old envelope a sepia-toned portrait of a young woman gazing unsmiling into the camera. Her face did not resemble any relative I knew. She was a very petite woman, no more than a girl really, with narrow shoulders and an impossibly slender waist. Her eyes were light, probably blue, and she looked very sweet and vulnerable. But I was struck by the tight curls on her head. Our family was known for straight, fine blond hair, so this girl was something of an outlier. On the back of the photograph was her name: Mary Ann Merrill, who I had been told was the mother of my grandmother, and my namesake. Years ago, my grandmother had given me a leather-bound book of poetry that had once been owned by Mary Ann Merrill, who'd signed her name on the title page. And here she was right in front of me: my great-grandmother.

There's something about the dress styles, hairdos, and posture of people in old photographs that seem comical to contemporary viewers. Sitting ramrod straight, with tight bodices that buttoned up to high collars, no makeup, dreadful hairdos, and not a flicker of a smile to soften the overall look, the portraits from the early days of photography seem to beg for a sassy caption. My brother, a born comedian, had plenty of comments for the occasion and poor Mary Ann Merrill was only the first of many targets for his jokes.

Drawn to the second pile, I dug into the trove of mementos and found one ancient tintype that almost took my breath away. Staring out from an image crackled with age was a fearsome looking woman, perhaps in her late thirties, with penetrating eyes, a stern mouth frozen into place by thin lips, her dark hair pulled back in a severe, no-nonsense style with tight ringlets tucked behind her ears. Dressed in a long black dress with a white lace collar tied tightly under her chin, she looked like a Dickensian school marm who carried a stick for beating small children. As I continued to study this old photograph, I was consumed with curiosity. Good grief, who *was* this woman? I assumed she and I were related on my father's side. I wondered how many generations separated us. When was she born, and when did she die? Who were her children, and how was she related to my father?

Staring at these two old photos was like opening a door just a bit on my parents' lives to catch a glimpse of those who preceded them. Here in my hands, I realized, was an entire family history I knew nothing about, people whose faces I did not recognize, most of whose names I did not know. Of course, a person's life is more than a snapshot in a photo album, a framed portrait on the wall, or even a tattered tintype discovered more than a century after it was taken. These people lived lives that were meaningful in every way and they deserved to be honored. Finding the "back story," I realized, was going to take some work.

Closing up that box, I committed to a decision that would take me on a fascinating journey. I vowed to return to the original family tree I started a few years before, crude and inaccurate as it was, and venture into some serious research. I joined Ancestry.com and started an online tree. I learned how to follow their genealogy "hints" and attach documents to my ancestors that "proved" the details of births, marriages and deaths. It was addicting, and I made more progress in two months than I'd made in two years of fiddling around with a hand-drawn family tree.

On both sides of my family, the Ancestry.com trail led to the United Kingdom – Lancashire in northern England on my mother's side, while my father's ancestors were firmly rooted in Cornwall in the extreme southwest of England.

Two years later, I had filled in many blanks on my family tree. Before I knew it, I was spitting into a vial to submit a DNA sample to another online service that took my lineage far, far back into the mists of early history. DNA analysis confirmed what the paper trail had revealed: Except for the occasional Dutchman, Frenchman or German, my ethnic ancestry is 96 percent from the British Isles. A second test confirmed that my haplogroup, or human family related to a single parent, is known as J1c7. It traces my maternal lineage back some 45,000 years to a distant hunter-gatherer migration from the Arabian Peninsula into the Near East and then Europe. My mother's genetic family surfaced in the British Isles about the time Stonehenge was built and was firmly entrenched among Celtic speakers in the British Isles about 4,000 years ago.

I had expected that this tidal wave of information would be profoundly moving to me, but it wasn't. However epic the scale of my genetic history was, it felt dreadfully impersonal. I had started my family history with the question, who am I? Was I supposed to be satisfied with the answer: J1c7?

My Merrill Namesake

I continued to stew over my genetic makeup but knew it wouldn't define me in a way that had any real meaning for me. The answer to the question, Who am I? lay in knowing the stories of my more immediate ancestors, my grandparents and great-grandparents, and not in speculating about my early human predecessors who lived thousands of years ago in a faraway land. Besides, no records exist for those folks; there's really no story to tell.

One day, as I once again studied that black-and-white photograph of Mary Ann Merrill, I decided, since we shared the same name, that she was a good place to start. After several weeks of online research, her story was revealed.

My maternal great-grandmother was born in Shelbina, Missouri, in 1875, the seventh child of Franklin Merrill and Rebecca Jane Raplee Merrill. When she was five, her mother died after giving birth to her ninth baby, a little boy who lived only a few weeks. Barely six months after her mother's death, her father remarried and little Mary Ann had a new stepmother, the twenty-four-year-old daughter of their neighbor.

As if the shock of losing a mother then having to accept a substitute wasn't enough for his seven

orphaned children, Franklin, and his new wife, looking for a fresh start, moved them all from Shelbina 235 miles west to Adair County, Iowa, in order to be near his brothers. It's easy to imagine those first years as a new family were fraught with emotional pain and difficult adjustments.

Ten years later, Mary Ann met twenty-three-year-old Emory Hall and on April 5, 1891, they married, although she was only fifteen and a half years old at the time. The ceremony took place at the Merrill family home and was officiated

Based on similar poses and photographic styles, it's safe to assume these photographs were taken on the same day by the same photographer. Both subjects wore formal clothing and matching white ribbons attached to their lapels. Mary Ann sported a corsage, signaling that she was the honoree of the occasion. This was surely their wedding day.

by a "minister of the gospel." Married at fifteen, pregnant at sixteen. I gazed at her wedding portrait and saw a vulnerable girl who was trading the remaining years of her childhood for motherhood. At age fifteen, I was a high school cheerleader and played left wing on the varsity field hockey team. I had a boyfriend, but marriage was not even a concept I could imagine. When I was fifteen, I still had years of education ahead of me. At age fifteen, Mary Ann had already finished her education. Like most nineteenth-century girls, Mary Ann had a short childhood. I was glad to find out that she had a long life. In my mind, that somehow made up for being a child bride.

Emory Aden Hall. I had already, as a child, fallen in love with this man's name. At some point in our childhood, our mother had taken my sister and me to Kansas where a large family reunion was held, and for the first time we heard that name. There is a certain cadence to chanting "EM-or-ee AY-den Hall" that was beguiling to our young ears. And when my sister and I inserted a third and invented name into the mix, we sang "Emory Aden Robinson Hall," giving us a catchy mantra for jumping rope and playing hopscotch. For years, I tried valiantly to find any document that could prove our great-grandfather had Robinson in his name, but to no avail. It was a real disappointment to both of us.

Mary Ann delivered her first child eleven months after her wedding back in her hometown of Shelbyville, and there she also delivered her second child, who would become my grandmother Golda Alice.

Mary Ann had her third child, a son, in Adair, Iowa. Then, around 1896, pregnant and with three small children in tow, Emory and Mary Ann purchased a farm 500 miles south and traveled to Woodward in Oklahoma Territory (Oklahoma didn't become a state until 1907) where a large contingent of the Merrill clan was homesteading. Mary Ann gave birth to three more children while living in Woodward. She was now the mother of six children and helping her husband run a farm.

It's not known why they decided to leave Oklahoma, but in 1905, Emory, Mary Ann and their children, now numbering eight, relocated to Fort Scott, some 350 miles northeast in the state of Kansas. Fort Scott at that time was an important railroad center in the Osage Plains about 90 miles south of Kansas City with a population of about 10,000 people. As the county seat for Bourbon County, Fort Scott had a vibrant economy centered on government, small industry and agriculture. But Emory never farmed again. When Emory brought his family there, he was thirty-seven-years-old and worked as a laborer "doing street work." Eventually, he worked for the Missouri Pacific Railroad in the shop where passenger and freight railcars were repaired, and he continued to do this work until his retirement.

Mary Ann had two more children in Fort Scott, the last one born when she was forty-three-years-old. With her brood numbering ten, she probably had precious little time for herself or community work. I'm sure it was a comfort and a help to her that so many of her relatives also lived in Fort Scott. Family gatherings must have been comically large, bursting with aunts and uncles and cousins.

Life in a small town is often idyllic. Children are free to ride bicycles everywhere, walk themselves to school, play in the street until dusk, and knock on their neighbor's back door at any hour. Parks and playgrounds are safe. Schools, churches and civic clubs are the center of social life. The downtown bustles with people going about their business and greeting each other on the way. I imagine this is how Emory, Mary Ann and their children lived in the early 1900s in Fort Scott.

I'm afraid time has not been kind to Fort Scott. I visited in 2017 and was overwhelmed with sadness. It is a town that is losing population and, I fear, opportunity. While there are a few exceptions, the downtown looked mostly abandoned and rundown. The stores and coffee shops had few customers. My footsteps echoed loudly on the empty sidewalks. The modest little frame homes appeared to be equally neglected, needing paint and new roofs. There was the feeling of desperation in the air, and part of me was glad that Emory and Mary Ann weren't around to see their little town struggling to survive.

Outside of town I found Evergreen Cemetery, the final resting place for Emory and Mary Ann and six of their ten children. Three more were buried nearby in the Fort Scott National Cemetery. Mary Ann died after suffering a heart attack at home in August 1952. She was seventy-six-years-old. Emory, who had been ill for a couple of years with hypertension, died of a cerebral hemorrhage four months later on New Year's Eve, December 31, 1952, at the age of eighty-four.

Mary Ann was just a girl when she married and had her first baby. She never had any education beyond the eighth grade and never worked outside the home. By today's expectations, her life would not draw much applause. But I think she deserves more credit than what can be seen through the lens of the twenty-first century. First, raising ten children is no small feat by anyone's standards. (In fact, Mary Ann gave birth to eleven children and lost one baby while she was still in her early twenties.) All her surviving children graduated from high school, a benchmark she never achieved for herself.

In the first half of the twentieth century, an era of limited transportation options for most, Emory and Mary Ann lived in four different states. For farm folk, wagons were the obvious choice. Trains were another. It is doubtful that this family of modest means owned an automobile, and certainly not one large enough to transport a large family and all their belongings. Travel must have been grueling, undertaken only with great determination and optimism. The decision to uproot and move hundreds of miles away was a very big step. Even within the same town, Emory and Mary Ann moved from house to house. In the forty-seven years they lived in Fort Scott, this restless pair moved four times.

And finally, I cannot overlook that book of William Wordsworth poems that my grandmother gave me after Mary Ann died in 1952. It is a hand-tooled leather-bound tome with gold leaf on the edges of all 700 pages, definitely not a textbook from any school. The first inside page bears the inked signature of "Miss Mary Merrill, Anita, Ia." Although she reveals that she was living in the little town of Anita in southwest Iowa, there is no date, but by using her maiden name, we know that Mary Ann signed it before her sixteenth birthday, and she kept that book for her entire life, bequeathing it to her daughter Golda Alice, my grandmother. I expect it was a gift from someone special. Tucked in between two pages at the back of the book was a tiny round paper sticker in the shape of a floral wreath with this message: "I will be true to thee." Could it have been a romantic gift from her future husband?

I think theirs was a real love story. Emory and Mary Ann were married for sixty-one years, were blessed with a large family, and lived long lives. Only death ended their union. In so many ways, it was an ideal life. But then, I am her namesake and that tends to bring out the sentimental side in me.

Mary Ann Merrill was my mom's grandmother, and it is for her that I was named, although my parents purloined Mary Ann's last name for my first name. I have spent my entire life spelling it and correcting the pronunciation of others, which varies from "MUR-ill" to "meh-RILL." Over the years, I have met one or two men named Merrill, but I have never run into any other woman with the same first name. (Meryl Streep doesn't count due to the different spelling.) As I dug further and further back into the Merrill line in my family tree, I was delighted to discover that we (last name) Merrills have an illustrious history dating back to Colonial America.

Nathaniel Merrill was born in 1601 in Suffolk County in England, married Susanna Wolterton, and together they emigrated to the British Colonies, landing in Ipswich, Massachusetts, in 1633. Nathaniel and Susanna were part of what is known as The Great Migration, that massive movement of some 20,000 British subjects seeking separation from the Church of England, which they viewed as corrupt. These Puritans, as they were known, crossed the Atlantic between the sailing of the Mayflower in 1620 and the outbreak of the English Civil War in 1640. In those twenty years, they settled dozens of colonies from Connecticut to Rhode Island to Massachusetts and southern Maine.

Nathaniel and Susanna lived some thirty miles north of Boston in neighboring Newbury, where they were given land to farm and raise livestock. Nathaniel died there in 1655 at the age of fifty-three. Together, they raised several children, who in turn spawned large families that populated towns throughout New England. When I lived in Maine it tickled me to see so many places carrying the Merrill name, but didn't know at the time that if I followed the genealogical thread, it would have led to a common ancestor, Nathaniel, the original immigrant.

On a New England trip a few years ago, I found the First Burying Ground of the Settlers tucked behind a copse of trees along the High Road in Newburyport, Massachusetts. Two members of the Merrill clan are buried there, including my eighth great-grandfather Nathaniel, whose headstone I was thrilled to find. Thanks to a community organization that keeps the cemetery in good shape, most of the original seventeenth-century headstones that had crumbled over time have been replaced with markers that are readable and hopefully they will last another few hundred years. All genealogists wish they could "meet" their ancestors in person. This was the day in 2012 when I did.

My sister Susan snapped this photo when I found our eight-times great-grandfather's headstone 247 years after his death in Newburyport, Massachusetts.

Franklin Merrill and Rebecca Jane Raplee

While researching my great-grandmother Mary Ann Merrill, I couldn't help but learn more and more about her parents and soon was eager to focus on that generation. Therein lies the addiction of genealogy: You can't stop.

I'd already learned that when Mary Ann was a very little girl, her mother had died just one week after giving birth to her ninth child. Her father, Franklin, my great-great-grandfather was left at the age of forty-one with seven children, ages five to seventeen. Just six months later, Franklin married Sophia Hamilton, the twenty-four-year-old daughter of a neighbor who became a surrogate mother to his large brood. Two months later, Franklin's nine-month-old son, John, died. In the span of two years he had lost a wife and two baby boys.

I wondered about this poor guy who'd experienced so much sadness and loss. Franklin was a farmer who had been born in 1839 in New Hampshire but had grown up in northwestern Illinois, on the border with Iowa. When he was twenty-three, he married twenty-one-year-old Rebecca Jane Raplee, who had been raised in a large family in western New York state. The

Raplee clan of upstate New York was massive and most of them lived their lives in the Finger Lakes region. That Rebecca left New York was surprising, and I wish her life had been a happier one.

For Rebecca and Frank, babies followed in rapid succession, as they predictably did in a time when birth control was non-existent. By the time he was thirty-five, Franklin had purchased 100 acres of farmland in Shelby County, Missouri, where he and Rebecca lived for many years. When she died, Franklin buried her next to the graves of their infant sons James Leslie and John Franklin. Thanks to the miracle of the internet, I found a photo of Rebecca's grave and was deeply saddened to see that her modest headstone had broken and crumbled into a heap of concrete debris. As a mother of nine children, I thought my great-great-grandmother Rebecca's memorial should be more heroic, and I silently castigated her surviving children who couldn't be bothered to keep her grave in better shape.

After Rebecca's death (she was only thirty-nine), I was shocked to learn that Franklin started courting Sophia Hamilton, a twenty-something neighbor, and six months later she moved into Frank's home. The newly configured family stayed in Adair County until 1900, when they moved to Woodward, Oklahoma.

Woodward is in the northwest corner of what was then Oklahoma Territory, where a number of the Merrill children had relocated when former

Indian lands were opened up by the United States government for homesteading. Franklin's daughter Mary Ann and her husband, Emory Hall, his son, Perry, and his wife, Eunice, and another daughter Nettie and husband, Eugene, were all there. Another two married daughters and their families lived nearby. It was a natural decision for a sixty-one-year-old man who may have tired of farming by then.

Franklin and Sophia were married for nine years until she died in 1900. Franklin buried her in Woodward in the Elmwood Cemetery. In very short order, Franklin remarried again. His third bride was none other than his daughter Mary Ann's mother-in-law, Naomi Wagoner Hall, who had been a widow for several years. Frank and Naomi lived in town where Franklin worked as a janitor in the local bank. When he died in 1918, he was eulogized in the local Methodist Church where he had worshipped for eighteen years. The local newspaper reported that he (affectionately known as "Uncle Frank") left four adult children in Woodward, plus two in Anita, Iowa, and my forty-two-year-old great-grandmother Mary Ann in Fort Scott, Kansas.

When I started my exploration into my great-great-grandfather's life, I reacted badly to what seemed like a very calculating move on his part: to remarry as soon as possible after the death of my great great-grandmother Rebecca. He and his kids could not have had adequate time to mourn Rebecca's death. Instead, he rushed into what I believed was a marriage of convenience. It seemed

This photograph of Franklin Merrill was taken in 1901 in Woodward, Oklahoma when he was seventy-two-years-old. At the time, he was married to Sophia, his second wife.

to be such a betrayal. And when his second wife died, true to form, he quickly married again.

But there was also another pattern emerging that led me to a different conclusion: Frank Merrill always put the welfare of his children first. When Rebecca died, he surely understood the urgency of re-creating a normal home life for his seven motherless children, and within six months, he had provided a substitute mother for them. And when his second wife died, Frank moved to Oklahoma where his grown children lived. This was a man who could not tolerate life on his own. He repeatedly turned to family.

In his long life of seventy-nine years, he produced nine children, seven of whom survived him. He stayed close to his children all his life, even when they were grown and had children of their own. He enjoyed three long marriages, and when he died, he left a fair amount of property to his widow and adult children. However success is measured – either as good health, reasonable financial comfort, the love of a family, or happiness – my great-great-grandfather seems to have done better than most, in spite of enduring much sadness as a younger man.

Joseph Speakman and Phoebe Anderton

We've all met someone who can boast, and usually does, about being "descended from the Mayflower." The claim is generally unsubstantiated, based vaguely on their cousin or uncle who "looked it up," proof enough for them, and intimidating enough of a statement to stop all further conversation in its tracks. To be able to claim an American pedigree back to 1620 is pretty darn impressive, I'll admit. I can't make the Mayflower claim, but 1633 is awfully close, thanks to Nathaniel and Susanna Merrill. The Merrill line is on my mother's maternal side, and they arrived in America almost 400 years ago. So, to anyone who asks me how long my people have been in this country, I can say with pride: ten generations. However, on my mother's paternal side of the family, the Speakmans, the immigrant to America arrived much later. My great-great-grandparents Joseph Speakman and Phoebe Anderton were both born and raised in Lancaster County in England, but only one of them lived to immigrate to the United States.

Lancashire is in northwest England flanked by the Irish Sea on the west and the county of Yorkshire on the east. At the time Joseph and Phoebe lived there, Lancashire had become quite industrialized with hundreds of coal mines and cotton mills. By the mid-nineteenth century, approximately 85 percent of all the cotton manufactured in the world was processed in Lancashire. Weaving cotton became a thriving cottage industry, employing thousands of poor laborers, entire families who toiled long hours over handlooms set up in their tiny dwellings to make cloth for the wealthier classes. Others, like Joseph, worked in the many collieries, or coal mines, that dotted the countryside.

Joseph was the fourth child and third son of his parents, John and Margery Speakman. He was born on June 11, 1824, and baptized like all the children in the Speakman family in St. Thomas Church. By the time he was fifteen, Joseph was working as a "drawer in a coal pit," meaning he worked near the opening of the mine shaft, dragging carts loaded with coal ore out into the open air where they were broken down into smaller usable chunks. Wages for underground work were very poor, paying about 40 pence for a six-day workweek of twelve-hour shifts. Wages for above-ground work were even less.

At age twenty-two, he married fifteen-year-old Mary Ann Fairhurst in the same church he was baptized in, and they had two children, Peter and Jane. The young couple lived with her parents in a small row house in the village of Haydock in the Lancaster parish of Ashton-in-Makerfield. In 1855, at the age of twenty-four, Mary Ann died of consumption, known today as tuberculosis, leaving Joseph with two small children.

A few years later, in 1860, Joseph married twenty-nine-year-old Phoebe Anderton in St. Thomas Church. Phoebe was the seventh of nine children born to her parents, Joseph Anderton and Rachel Roby. She lived at home in the village of Billinge, working as a hand weaver alongside her parents and siblings. She likely never attended school because when she and Joseph married, she signed the church register with an "X," indicating she was illiterate.

In 1862, their son, John, was born, and two years after that, in 1864, Joseph was dead at the age of thirty-nine, another victim of "consumption." Consumption, now known as tuberculosis, took the lives of thousands of British mine workers.

Phoebe was then a thirty-two-year-old widow with two stepchildren and a toddler of her own to support. It is not known how she managed to survive, but we do know that she was enticed by her older sister Lavinia's new life in the American state of Illinois. Peter, then twenty, and Jane, then fifteen, opted to remain in England. And so it was that in 1868 Phoebe left the port of Liverpool and set sail to New York with five-year-old John, escorted by Lavinia's husband, George Gee. Together, they made their way to Illinois and a new life, thus bringing the Speakman line to America.

One day not long ago, as I reached far back into the Anderton line on my online family tree, I discovered someone from England who was also researching my fourth great-grandfather Joseph

Anderton (1754-1827). Fascinated, I sent her an email, and after several exchanges, we found that we are fourth cousins. Jenny, my new-found relative, disclosed to me that her mother's maiden name was Anderton, making her mom, Gillian, my third cousin. But that wasn't all. In a stroke of remarkable luck, Gillian and her husband, John, spent every winter in Palm Springs, California, only a few hours' drive from my home! The following February, I was in the car headed to a much-anticipated meeting with my new British cousins. It was a lovely, warm visit, and we repeated that winter ritual the following year. And the year after that, I made a trip to Cornwall to investigate the Tippett line. Before I left to go home, I spent a delightful few days with Gillian and John, as well as Jenny's family, in Devonshire, just north of Cornwall, where they all live. Last year, Jenny and her family came to California for a tour of the state, and my son Eric met them in Santa Cruz; I hosted them in Ojai and Ventura a few days later. Another joy of genealogy is finding family and making new friends.

In this photo, John Speakman looks to be about five or six years old. It may have been taken in Lancashire just prior to their leaving for America. Or a few months later when they arrived in Illinois. Even as a youngster, John was strikingly handsome with blond curls and intense eyes.

Her new American home was LaSalle County in north central Illinois, sixty miles west of the city of Chicago. Two events were key in

Photo of young John Speakman at the knee of his mother, Phoebe Speakman.

developing this part of the American heartland, formerly known as the Northwest Territory: the completion of the Erie Canal that linked New York state to the Great Lakes in 1825, and the end of the Black Hawk Indian wars in 1832 that had curtailed westward expansion by white pioneers from New England and New York state. By 1868 when Phoebe arrived, she found farms carved out of the dense virgin forest and wild prairie that were now connected by roads and a river that provided a means for transporting livestock and crops to the city.

Within two months of her arrival in the United States, Phoebe was married to Duncan Hamilton, a Scottish immigrant who had settled into small-town life in the village of Vermilion, Illinois, in the 1850s. It is possible that Phoebe's sister, Lavinia, and brother-in-law, George Gee, had this match all but arranged before she arrived. An eligible forty-one-year-old bachelor and a thirty-seven-year-old widow with a child would make the perfect pair in the eyes of well-meaning relatives, or so they perhaps thought. Whatever the motivations, Phoebe and Duncan presented themselves to the Justice of the Peace in LaSalle County on April 30, 1868, and became husband and wife.

According to the 1870 Census, Phoebe was "keeping house" and her husband ran a grocery store in Vermilion. By 1880, the three were living on a farm just outside of Lowell, a village of seventy-seven inhabitants. Phoebe's son, John, then seventeen, listed his occupation as a farm laborer. The Illinois state agricultural schedule for that year is almost unreadable but verifies that Duncan Hamilton owned about thirty acres that produced livestock and various crops.

We can only imagine how very different her American life was from her former British life. No longer living in crowded terrace houses in industrial Lancashire, she enjoyed the expansive views of the American prairie with fresh air, clean running creeks and rivers, and quaint farm towns. And yet, life in rural Illinois had some surprising similarities. LaSalle County at that time had abundant coal seams and many early settlers worked in the mines. The 1870 Census enumerated several of Phoebe and Duncan's neighbors who were coal miners. Although it must have been a pleasant life in many ways, rural women worked hard and were often isolated on farms outside of town. She had Lavinia nearby, but surely there were times when Phoebe desperately missed her Lancashire family and her English way of life.

It is a tragedy that the entire 1890 U.S. Census was lost in a great warehouse fire, leaving a huge gap in information about more than sixty-two million Americans. Consequently, nothing is known today about Phoebe and her family for almost twenty years. We can imagine they continued living in the same place doing the same things, raising livestock, growing crops, and making much of their own food and clothing. But there is always so much more to a person's life than Census data reports. As a resident of Victorian America, what social changes did she witness taking place in her new home? Was she active in her community or her church? As a woman, she was not able to vote, but did she follow the politics of the day? Did she learn to read the newspaper? Did she record her opinions in a diary or in letters back home to her family? What new inventions of the day made their way into her life? Did she learn how to use a cash register, a sewing machine, an electric mixer, an iron or a manual can opener? She lived in an age of rapid change and social upheaval, and we don't know anything about what part she played in it.

Phoebe died in winter 1892 at the relatively young age of sixty-one and was buried in the cemetery in Lowell, Illinois. In yet another example of how women often lived – and died – in obscurity, no obituary was submitted to the local newspaper. In the January 30 edition of the Tonica News, three days after she died, one short paragraph reported that the editors had just learned of the death of Mrs. Duncan Hamilton (they don't even use her first name), and promised, "A suitable notice of the deceased will appear next week." No article ever appeared in subsequent editions. To this day, the cause of her death is not known. I do not doubt that her husband, Duncan, and her son, John, must have grieved deeply at the passing of their wife and mother. But it is incomprehensible that an acknowledgment of her life went without public notice. Compared to the style in which Duncan's funeral was comported thirteen years later, poor Phoebe appeared to have been considered a mere footnote in that family's life.

A few months after Phoebe's death, Duncan moved to Ohio where he met and married Caroline Tucker in 1894. He died there in 1905 at the age of seventy-eight. After a funeral in Ohio, his body was brought back to Lowell for a second service. Duncan, who had served three years in the 42nd Illinois Infantry during the Civil War and was gravely wounded by a musket ball in his chest, was given full military honors with members of the Grand Army of the Republic (Union vets from the Civil War) serving as pallbearers. His obituary in the newspaper was extensive. He was buried next to Phoebe with a very modest headstone but was officially awarded a special military headstone in 1939, thirty-four years after his death. Whoever was responsible for bestowing this honor is unknown.

Phoebe Anderton Speakman Hamilton. She had the courage and gumption to travel almost 4,000 miles from her place of birth to start a new life in a foreign country. She lived sixty-one years as a daughter, wife, mother, widow and wife again, but was known only for "keeping house."

When Phoebe and John arrived on U.S. soil in 1868, they brought the Speakman line to America. They also placed the Speakmans firmly in the Midwest where their descendants still live today. Studying four generations of my mother's ancestors took me on virtual journeys to Ohio, Illinois, Iowa, Missouri, Kansas and Oklahoma.

It's hard to imagine how genealogists did their work before the Internet. They surely spent hours and hours writing letters and research requests to local libraries, telephoning and patiently interviewing total strangers, crashing into lots of dead ends. Some of my favorite moments in this entire process are conversations I had with volunteers at local historical societies. Without exception, these men and women, usually older folks who know every detail about their towns, are anxious to help and devote hours poring over old newspapers to find a tidbit of news about your ancestor. Then they photocopy announcements of graduations, engagements, weddings, funerals and military service and carefully mail a packet, a treasure trove, to you. These small historical societies usually have a budget of zero; they're offering their services because, well, that's what they do. To repay them in some small way, I have purchased memberships in historical societies all over the Midwest and am proud to do what I can to keep them in the business of preserving their history – and mine.

Only four months after his mother's death, John married a local girl, Maude Eudella Stofer, and they set up household next door to her father, Benjamin Stofer, a widower. John and Maude's first child, Glendon Clyde Speakman, my grandfather, was born later that year. Five more children followed in rapid succession. Around 1901, John and Maude moved the family to Fort Scott, Kansas, where their seventh and last child, Gladys, was born.

The 1910 Census reports the family living on a horse farm in Fort Scott, which tickled me

According to the photographer's imprint on this photograph, the picture was taken in Tonica, Illinois, where John and Maude were married. This may have been their formal wedding portrait.

because it seemed to explain my grandfather's love of horses. If indeed he was raised around horses and learned to handle them, then it was natural that in his adult life, he would own horses.

To my dismay, a few years later they were found living in Stuart, Florida, thirty-eight miles north of West Palm Beach. This discovery was so out of character for the Speakmans that I kept ignoring the entries in the Palm Beach city directories, until the 1920 Census confirmed that they owned a horse farm in Stuart. I have no idea what took my great-grandfather all the way from Kansas to Florida, so far from everything he knew. Yet there he was. He was fifty-eight-years-old and he and Maude had relocated with three of their children. My grandfather, Glen, the eldest, had already left home and married my grandmother.

John and Maude continued to live in Florida unti l her death in 1925, when he returned to Fort Scott, Kansas. Shortly thereafter, he moved into Glen's house in Kansas City to live with my grandmother Golda and their two children, my mother, Glenda, and my Uncle Jack.

John died of a heart attack in 1935 when he was seventy-three-years-old. He was buried in Fort Scott next to his wife, Maude.

On a cold and dreary early spring morning several years ago, I drove from Kansas City to Fort Scott, the town that was home to so many of my Speakman relatives. There's a small section near a large tree with a prominent headstone with just one name on it, Speakman. Clustered all around are the graves of numerous family members: spouses, children, and siblings. It was a very moving experience for me to know they'd all come home at the end of their lives.

I had a nice visit with the groundskeeper at Evergreen Cemetery, who showed me a hand-drawn map of all the gravesites of the large Speakman clan. He seemed to know the married names of the Speakman women, and even offered to contact the few Speakman descendants who still lived in Fort Scott. I wish I'd had more time to take him up on his generous offer, but I had a plane to catch and didn't dare linger too long.

It saddens me to know that no more Speakmans will likely be buried there in the future. We've all moved away and live in faraway places we now call home.

Glendon Clyde Speakman and Golda Alice Hall

My grandfather Glendon Clyde Speakman was born on Christmas Day 1892 in Lowell, Illinois. When he was ten, his parents John and Maude left north central Illinois and moved five hundred miles south to Fort Scott, Kansas. By then, Glen had six younger siblings, and in 1915 when he turned twenty-two, he left the family farm to rent a room in town and become the proprietor of the Fort Scott Cleaners & Dyers. The store soon evolved into a men's haberdashery, selling suits, ties, and hats That same year, he married my grandmother, Golda Alice Hall.

It was, according to the local newspaper, a beautiful wedding. "Miss Hall was gowned in a beautiful dress of white crepe de chine, made with silk overlace and trimmings of pearl. Her long veil descended from a wreath of lilies of the valley...The church was decorated for the occasion in a profusion of ferns and other greenery." Unfortunately, I never found a photograph from Nana's wedding day. The reason would eventually become clear.

Golda and Glen holding baby Glenda at five weeks old.

A few years later, Glen joined the sales team at Butler Steel Works, and he and Golda moved from Fort Scott to corporate headquarters in Kansas City. Butler was a big company that was known for numerous products of rolled steel: silos, grain storage bins, and stock feed bins. Glen continued to advance in his career at Butler and he eventually had to move his young family to Philadelphia while he managed a very large territory along the Eastern seaboard. By 1930, Golda and Glen had moved their daughter, Glenda, now thirteen, and son, Jack, eight, back to Kansas City when Glen was named sales manager at the rapidly growing company now called Butler Manufacturing Company. His annual salary by 1940 had reached an impressive $5,000, about $90,000 in today's dollars.

By 1935, however, my grandparents' marriage had faltered and Golda, then in her forties, had moved with her son and daughter to an apartment on West 48th Street in downtown Kansas City. Glen rented a room on Ward Parkway with another salesman from Butler. Understandably, the next few years were difficult. Golda surprised everyone by taking my mother Glenda and my uncle Jack to Miami, Florida, where they spent a few months getting away from all the stress of the divorce.

However, one grand event happened in Florida: my mother met my father. For a couple of glorious weeks, the three Speakmans were wined and dined by Russ Tippett, an impressive bachelor from New York who was determined to court the twenty-year-old Glenda.

It was in Miami that this Midwestern family was introduced to fish, lobster, pizza and exotic cocktails at all the finest restaurants and nightclubs. By the time the three Speakmans returned to Kansas City, Glenda was making wedding plans. My mother and dad exchanged vows in Kansas City in 1940 and moved to the suburbs of New York City.

In February 1942, Glen, then forty-nine, married thirty-three-year-old Berry Briddelle Smith of Kansas City. Their son, Glendon Caldwell Speakman, was born in December 1943, a year after I was born. Technically, Glendon is my half-uncle, even though he is younger than I am. I know my mother never got used to referring to Glendon as her half-brother, and I admit I struggled with seeing him as my half-uncle. In

This is the oldest photo I have ever seen of my parents together. It was probably taken in Florida in the early days of their courtship.

recent years, Glendon and I have shared a laugh over that, but there's an awkwardness that lingers all the same.

I can remember visiting my grandfather and "Aunt Briddelle," as we called her, in their large brick house in Kansas City. Granddad had become a prominent figure in the community. Quite the civic leader, Glen was active in Rotary International, the Shriners and the Masons. Glendon remembers watching with his mother whenever his dad rode with the Masons in holiday parades, resplendent in bright riding attire atop a saddle sparkling with silver decorations. Glen also served on boards for the Kansas City Art Institute and the Baptist Memorial Hospital for many years. By the time he retired in 1957, Granddad was vice president of sales and advertising for all national and international operations of this iconic steel manufacturing company.

In retirement, he returned to an interest from his youth: breeding horses. One of his horses, Stormy Weather, a black and white paint, was a three-time world champion in parade class that he trained to perform in the 3-gaited and 5-gaited divisions, an unusual accomplishment for that breed. When I was a little girl, I was privileged to present a silver trophy to Stormy Weather, who had been selected Best in Parade Class in the show ring in front of thousands of cheering fans at Kansas City's prestigious American Royal. Granddad soon built an impressive collection of very expensive show saddles and bridles, all hand-tooled leather with silver-clad horns and stirrups, and dozens of silver trophies and blue ribbons, which he proudly displayed in his home.

My grandfather was a committed Christian and a life-long member of the Methodist Church, who brooked no excuses to avoid attending church. Once, while visiting him in Kansas City, he scolded me roundly for pleading some kind of vague malaise on Sunday morning as the rest of his family was dressing for church. I insisted that my stomach ache was real and got to stay home, even though he knew I was "welching," as he put it. I've always regretted that show of childish stubbornness. Granddad got cheated out of showing off his granddaughter to his friends, and I missed out sharing with him something he held dear.

On a happier note, I hold an abiding memory of my grandfather's generosity. When I was a small child living in suburban New York, my parents roused us three kids out of bed one morning to witness an unusual delivery. Idling in the front of our house was a huge truck with a 10-foot diameter steel bin strapped down to the flatbed. On the side, stamped in blue letters, was "Butler Manufacturing Company." Granddad had shipped it all the way from Kansas City to his New York grandchildren, but we didn't understand why. We were told it was actually a watering trough for cows. To an audience of curious neighbors and bedazzled kids, the gigantic bin was rolled noisily across our driveway to the back yard where it was put into position next to our swing set. Later that afternoon, the local hardware store filled it with sand, and we had the grandest sandbox in Bronxville, New York!

Although Granddad lived a vigorous and active life, as he entered his sixties, he developed heart problems and suffered several heart attacks before he retired. He died on November 15, 1973, at the age of eighty, and I'm sure his funeral at the Country Club Methodist Church was magnificent, a fitting farewell to a dedicated church leader.

Even though they continued to live in the same city, my grandparents went their separate ways after their divorce in 1941. Golda started using her middle name and became known as Alice. She began a successful career in real estate sales and by 1956 was named president of the Women's Division of the real estate board. She used her considerable musical talent to sing with the choir of the Central Methodist Church and perform with the Kansas City chapter of the Sweet Adelines, an international organization of women singers who specialize in barbershop harmony.

Most summers, Nana visited my childhood home in New York. She attended my debutante ball in 1960 and my wedding in 1965. She was present when I brought home my first baby, her first great-grandchild, in 1967. I remember her gentle voice, soft with Southern inflections, and her quaint way of drawing out the syllables of certain words that my ears had only heard in a clipped East Coast staccato. Nana died on February 23, 1969, and was buried in her childhood hometown of Fort Scott, Kansas.

While my grandparents' lives were remarkable in many ways, I was struck by the sheer size of the families in which they were raised. My Nana was the second of ten children born to Emory and Mary Ann Hall. As the second-oldest child,

Golda Alice Speakman in 1956

and a girl at that, she welcomed a new brother or sister every two or three years. I am sure she assumed many duties of mothering at an early age, like diapering, feeding and watching over an ever-increasing brood.

It saddens me that I did not know any of her brothers or sisters, even though only two of them had passed away before I was born. I have a very vague memory of being at a family reunion as a child many years ago but cannot remember meeting any of my great aunts or uncles. I don't recall my mother talking about her mother's siblings much, if at all. But I do remember Nana, when asked, rapidly reciting their names with a twinkle in her eye. To me, that was an amazing feat. She had five sisters and four brothers, while I had only one of each.

My grandfather Glen was the eldest of seven children born to John and Maude Speakman, five boys and two girls. Like my grandmother, he saw a new sibling born every couple of years, but as a boy, he was probably absolved of any child care duties. I don't recall ever meeting any of them, even though all but one was still alive all the years I was growing up, attending college, getting married and having children of my own. Although I grew up halfway across the country, it's still hard for me to understand, so many years later, why so many relatives were complete strangers to me. I'm grateful today that technology has provided me a glimpse into their lives.

Glen and Golda Alice Speakman, my maternal grandparents, were the first on this side of my family to divorce. Back in 1941, it was fairly unusual and still not acceptable. I think my mother carried a certain resentment toward her father and his new family throughout her adult life. I can remember feeling the unspoken tension whenever they were mentioned. Since then, I have endured my own divorce and I'm sure my two children could make the same statement about feeling the tension, avoiding certain topics of conversation, and learning how to stay neutral and just grin and bear it. The insidious result of divorce is wounds that are not brought to light and never allowed to heal. In a long-ago conversation with my mother's brother, Jack, I heard him refer to Glendon – the child of Glen and Briddelle – as his "brother." How about that, I thought. They were twenty-two years apart in age, and technically speaking, they were half-brothers who were never raised together but shared the same father. But his words sounded like genuine forgiveness and acceptance to me, and I salute Jack for making that happen.

My Parents, James Russell Tippett and Glenda Alice Speakman

My mother was born in Fort Scott, Kansas, and spent her childhood there with her mother, father and younger brother, Jack. When she was a young teenager, her father moved the family to Kansas City, where he started working as a salesman for Butler Manufacturing Company. Her father's widowed father, John Speakman, moved with the family into a large rented house on Bellefontaine Avenue. She graduated from Southwest High School and attended University of Kansas in Lawrence, where she majored in music theory.

My mother always told the story of the night when Tommy and Jimmy Dorsey, whose touring band was all the rage at that time, arrived on the K.U. campus to entertain the students. During one of the performances, she was asked to sing on stage with them. Apparently, she impressed the Dorsey brothers because they asked her if she'd like to go on the road and tour with them. But, alas, her father wouldn't hear of it, telling her, "Nice girls don't do that."

Parental restraints notwithstanding, my mother went on to spend her entire life in the world of music, not as a touring professional, but as a volunteer arranger and director for women's choral groups. At one time, I remember her juggling the demands of rehearsing and performing with five different groups in Westchester County, New York, where I grew up. Their specialty was standards, songs of established popularity but arranged with a unique sound that she wrote in four-part harmony for women's voices. Her groups trooped to hospitals, convalescent homes, veterans' homes and even prisons. They performed at gala events and holiday balls. I recall Mom carrying around a tote bag of sheet music to our tennis club during the summer, and in between matches, she'd find a quiet spot in the shade away from the crowd and sit down by herself to arrange music. It was always a mystery to me how she could write music without a piano. But sure enough, back home later that day, she'd sit at the piano to test the notes she'd written, and it would sound exactly as she had heard it in her head.

It has been my life-long shame and frustration that I did not inherit but a tiny smattering of my mother's talents. Mom made me take piano lessons as a child, which I hated. And I hated my piano teacher who faithfully showed up at our house every week to oversee her pouty and unmotivated student, who had put in minimal practice time and never developed a feel or a love for my assigned pieces. In the evenings, when Mom was in the kitchen preparing dinner for the family, I'd be plopped at the piano slogging my way through some melody, and my mother, who had perfect pitch, would call from the kitchen, "B flat, Merrill! Can't you hear it has to be B flat?" I am sure my lack of talent at the piano was my mother's life-long shame and frustration as well. I had just enough musicality in my bones that I was recruited to sing in a long string of choruses from childhood through college. To this day, I treasure those experiences and still recall the lyrics and the alto part to many choral standards: The "Hallelujah Chorus" from Handel's "Messiah," "The Battle Hymn of the Republic," old spirituals like "There Is A Balm in Gilead," most hymns ever sung in the Presbyterian church, and all Christmas carols. It is not a vast repertoire, I admit, but that's the music that was sung in schools and churches in the 1950s.

By the time my mother reached her twenties, her parents' marriage was failing. Inexplicably, my grandparents made the decision to send my Uncle Jack off to military school in Georgia. The poor kid, only 16 years old, was put on a train and shipped off to the East Coast. Years later, Jack would say there was never any family conversation about this, that he was simply told that the next day he was leaving, and he was too intimidated to ask questions. When I heard this, it broke my heart. My mother was finishing her last year of college in Lawrence, so Nana left the family home to live in a downtown apartment in Kansas City. Not long after, she took them both to Miami to escape the stress. Jack was uprooted again and spent a semester in the local high school in Florida. It was there that twenty-three-year-old

In this photo, my mother is wearing the shell pink wedding dress that my sister, Susan, and I found in the attic of her home when we were closing down the house for sale after her death. It broke our hearts to have to toss it out, but years and years in a cardboard box had destroyed the fabric beyond redemption.

Glenda met thirty-two-year-old Russ Tippett, a young executive from the New York publishing world. It must have been love at first sight, because their engagement was quickly announced, and a wedding date was set for September 21, 1940, in the Country Club Methodist Church in Kansas City.

James Russell Tippett, my father, was born in Grass Valley in California's mining country. His parents, George Henry and Corinda, must have been surprised when this last baby arrived, fifteen years after their first child, George, and twelve and ten years after his sisters Jane and Anne. The family moved to San Francisco where he attended Lowell High School, and where his father died in 1924 when my dad was only sixteen. He attended San Mateo Junior College, then transferred to Stanford in 1932 to study pre-med, but never completed his degree. It was the depths of the Great Depression, and he made the decision to seek his fortune on the East Coast. By 1935, when he was twenty-seven, he had made his way to New York and was employed as a circulation manager at Dell Publishing Company. He lived in Brooklyn with a guy named Bob Barrett, who would remain a lifelong friend. On a business trip to Florida in 1940, he met my mother, Glenda, and they were married within the year.

My newlywed parents set up housekeeping in a duplex in suburban New York. Fifteen months later, in 1941, Pearl Harbor was bombed and the United States entered World War II. Nine and a half months later, I was born, and six months after that my father enlisted in the U.S. Navy as a lieutenant junior grade, and the new family moved to Arlington, Virginia. My sister, Susan, was born there in 1944. Dad was honorably discharged from the Navy in 1945, and my parents returned to civilian life and purchased what became my childhood home in Bronxville, New York.

When going through my parents' papers after their deaths many years later, I was fascinated at how closely their real estate transactions mirrored the postwar economic boom. They bought their first house at 3 Brassie Lane for $11,000, then sold it eight years later in 1953 for $30,000. Even after paying off that mortgage and covering closing costs, they made a tidy profit. Then they purchased their second home at 17 Course View Road for $42,000 and sold it in 1988 for $662,500. Their final real estate investment was in Ojai, California, which they bought for $275,000 in 1988, and their Trust sold it after their deaths for $650,000.

My dad spent his entire career in the publishing industry. He started at Dell, publishers of sewing pattern books and paperback novels. He moved on to Hearst Corporation, publishers of a line of women's magazines including *Good Housekeeping, Cosmopolitan, Seventeen* and others. Every morning, he would commute on the train to Grand Central Terminal in Midtown Manhattan, and every evening my mother would pick him up at the Bronxville station. The train trip took twenty-eight minutes each way, just enough time to peruse the morning and evening papers or unwind in the bar car from a hectic day in the city.

At the dinner table, he would regale us with stories about the demanding editors and publishers who behaved outrageously and offended everyone around them. My father, raised in laid-back California, had an easy-going temperament, and how he tolerated those brash New Yorkers, I'll never understand. But he could mimic each one of them in a way that made us laugh. In the mid-'60s, the upstart author of *Sex and the Single Girl*, Helen Gurley Brown, took over as editor of *Cosmo*, as it was known. She had no previous editorial experience, but she was determined to revamp the magazine, which was written by men, into a women's magazine with a woman's perspective. You can imagine the uproar that caused at Hearst. Even though my dad worked on the circulation side of the magazine, not the editorial side, Ms. Gurley Brown — all 100 pounds of her — was a force of nature and had all those men in a tizzy.

My father had a passion for sailing. I don't know where or when he learned to skipper a boat, but he finally purchased a twenty-eight-foot sloop that he named the Linda Lee, borrowing the middle names of his two daughters. My mother would pack a large thermos of her signature blend of half iced tea and half orange juice, and off we'd go to the boatyard in Mamaroneck, New York, where he moored his little blue sailboat. One gorgeous summer day, when I was about twelve, he and I took the boat for a day sail on Long Island Sound. Conditions were perfect, just enough breeze to keep us moving along at a nice clip, and no chop to make things challenging. He urged me to take the tiller, and he slid down low in the cockpit to relax and keep an eye on how I was managing. It was glorious. I felt like a carved mermaid on the bowsprit of an eighteenth-century vessel with the wind blowing my hair back and just letting the wind and the water carry me on. We passed a family in their boat, and I waved and looked for all the world like I was in total control. They, of course, did a double take to see this little girl skippering a fair-sized boat all alone, no one else in sight. My father and I told that story over and over again, and here it is being retold yet again.

In 1954, my dad made the decision to leave the publishing world and started working for Walt Disney, who was finalizing plans for a theme park in Southern California. Dad was put in charge of sales for the concessions on the park's Main Street. He landed contracts from Minute Maid, Pendleton, Kodak, and many others, who saw the huge potential for their product lines in this one-of-a-kind park. In summer 1955, our family moved to Orange County, where we rented a fantastic house on Lido Isle in Newport Beach while my father worked feverishly to meet the opening deadline. The private opening of the park in mid-July 1955 was reserved for employees and their families, and we spent an incredible day as VIPs in the Magic Kingdom. I met Walt Disney himself, but the highlight of the day for me was shaking hands with Fess Parker, who was dressed in full regalia as Davy Crockett.

Dad's stint at Disney was short-lived, since after the park opened there was no further need for new concession sales. He returned to the New York publishing world as vice president and circulation director at McCall Corporation, publisher of *McCall's Magazine, Redbook, Popular Mechanics* and other titles. Known as one of the Seven Sisters of women's magazines in the 1950s and 1960s, *McCall's* peaked at 8.5 million in circulation in its heyday. I can remember my father talking about Herb Mayes, who came in as the new editor in 1958 and drastically redesigned the magazine. So Herb Mayes joined the pantheon of characters around our dinner table. But after Mayes retired in 1965, the magazine lost its way and was eventually discontinued.

1965 was the year I got married and moved away from my parents' house in New York, and I essentially lost touch with my father's career from that time on. I do know that he was no longer associated with any of the big publishing houses in Manhattan and that our basement was filled with books he would ship out to various distribution centers. Working independently was stressful for him and took a toll on his health. By the mid-1980s, they were seriously thinking about selling the house in Bronxville and moving to Ojai to be near me. It didn't surprise me. Every year, on the morning of the first snowfall of the season, my father would go out on his front porch and mutter, "Goddamn it." This man from California had never gotten used to the bitter cold of East Coast winters, and he yearned to leave it all behind.

And so they did. In 1988, they purchased a charming house in a lovely neighborhood in semi-rural Ojai where my dad could sit in his new back yard and gaze at the mountains that surround the Ojai Valley. To him, those foothills could have been the Rockies. He marveled at their barrenness and stark beauty and how their colors changed throughout the day from dark blue gray to pink to lavender. He joined the Retired Men's Club and regaled the old gents with war stories from his life in New York City.

After a few years, Dad was diagnosed with multiple myeloma and eventually moved into a convalescent facility. He died in 1992 when he was eighty-three years old. We buried him in the scruffy little Ojai cemetery, just a few feet from Ojai's legendary Chumash elder, which my brother observed would have pleased our dad no end. Dad was fascinated with the lore of the Ojai Valley's first inhabitants and we agreed that lying in rest next to a grave decorated with feathers, shells and beads would have delighted him.

My mother remained in the house and continued with her music, arranging and directing her new local group, Class Act. One Independence Day morning, while standing on the curb to watch Ojai's ragtag parade, I looked up at a large float to see my own mother sitting at a keyboard playing a familiar melody, with the Class Act ladies singing their hearts out behind her. To my eternal regret, I was too stunned to take a photo, but I clearly remember catching her eye and seeing her nod at me with a mischievous look on her face. When I recovered from the shock, I thought, "Well, why not?" She was the embodiment of the book *When I Am an Old Woman, I Shall Wear Purple*. Three cheers, Mom.

One day, while Class Act was rehearsing at Mom's house, she suffered a stroke. It robbed her of enough of her cognitive abilities that she was unable to pick up her music again and the group disbanded. When my siblings and I finally had to move her into a facility, we made sure her piano went with her. She would occasionally sit down and play, but it was mere fragments of songs, little riffs on the keys that came from muscle memory more than any cerebral effort. Some days, I'd take her on drives through town to revisit all her old haunts and I'd play a CD of her arrangements. She'd start tapping her toes to get the beat going, smile softly at me and declare, "Ooh, that's so good!"

Mom lived to be ninety-two, but she left us years before then. End-stage dementia eventually took its toll, and it was agonizing for me. It broke my heart when she no longer recognized me, when she couldn't remember to swallow her food, when she couldn't speak. She and my father lie next to each other in the little Ojai cemetery in the shadow of the mountains they both adored.

Eva Jane Tippett

My father never talked much about his family. His own father died when Dad was just sixteen, I barely remembered his mother, who died when I was nine, and I never heard anything about his sister Anne or his brother, George. Fifteen years apart in age, he and George had little in common. When George died in California, my dad was married and living in New York. I doubt he even went to his brother's funeral. But I certainly knew his sister Jane, who lived in Washington, D.C., and visited us often, usually for holiday weekends.

For my sister and me, a visit from Aunt Jane was great fun. She always had a smile on her face and her pale blue eyes twinkled when she grinned. She had a high-pitched voice and her laugh resembled a screech. Like my father, she dropped her R's in a way that sounded slightly foreign to me. I always thought she wore too much makeup and could hardly take my eyes off her lipstick, which was bright red and went beyond the natural outline of her lips to make her mouth look more voluptuous. She penciled her eyebrows into a high arc, so she always appeared slightly surprised. With blond soft curls that framed her face, she looked like a kewpie doll.

This is a very old photo of Aunt Jane on one of her trips to visit our family in Bronxville. It was taken back in the years my parents owned a woodie station wagon, probably in the early 1950s.

Without saying a word, my mother made it clear she did not approve of Aunt Jane. Mom was not above rolling her eyes when Jane was talking, a gesture I hope was not noticed by Jane. Aunt Jane, who was not married when I knew her, went by the sort of French-sounding name of Jane Bruné, but none of us kids ever knew who her supposed husband was. When we asked, three things happened: We were told his name was Ray Bruné, Mom rolled her eyes, and the subject was abruptly dropped.

Aunt Jane drove a car she named Gwendolyn and kept a Meerschaum pipe on her dashboard. One summer, I was sent to Washington to visit her, and she bought me a small ragdoll to play with. The doll was black, had yarn dreadlocks, and sported a red bandana. I named her Magnolia Blossom and kept her for years until my doll-playing years were over, but I remember that little doll vividly.

Aunt Jane attended my wedding, looking sharp in a knee-length silk dress that showed off her shapely legs. She had long fingernails, very fair skin and no muscle tone. Never one to spend much time outdoors, Jane didn't take walks and had no interest in joining our family at our swim and tennis club. She was the definition of a hothouse flower. It would be years and years before I knew who this delicate violet really was.

Eva Jane Tippett, my father's older sister, was born in the California foothills in the little mining town of Grass Valley. In all my research, no official record of her birth was ever found, but in the U.S. Censuses from 1900, 1910, 1920 and 1930 she was called Eva and her birth was recorded in 1896. Most of the time my father called her "Eva," which always surprised the rest of the family because to us she was Jane. I know from old newspaper articles that she and her siblings Anne and George spent their formative years in Grass Valley attending the little elementary school there.

When Jane was in her early twenties, the Tippett family moved to San Francisco where she found work as a stenographer. Her father died when she was twenty-seven. One year later, in 1924, she married John Preston Garry. Her younger brother, Russell, my father who was sixteen at the time, and her aunt Annie Wicks were witnesses at their City Hall wedding. A little research revealed that Garry, a private in the U.S. Army, had been wounded in 1918 on the Western front and was hospitalized in France. He returned to California to convalesce, married my aunt, but within several years the marriage faltered and Aunt Jane filed for divorce. He died on February 17, 1929, just four days after the divorce decree was finalized. Thirty-three years old and newly divorced, Jane started using her maiden name again and moved in with her mother and brother George. In the 1930 Census she claimed she was a widow, not a divorcee.

I found myself obsessing about Aunt Jane's earlier years because in our family, those details were never discussed. My father was maddeningly vague and my mother stayed sourly mute. I was convinced they were hiding something. And, it turns out, they were. Never once did either of them mention Aunt Jane's marriage to John Garry, but my father's signature was right on the marriage certificate, and he actually lived for a while with Jane and John Garry when he was eighteen years old! All these years later, I still don't understand why that fact was so secret, although my parents clearly disapproved of how things played out. But it was going to get worse, much worse.

Jane worked at various jobs, including helping out in her brother George's new medical office in San Francisco. She also did sales work for KSAN, a San Francisco radio station. It was here that I believe Aunt Jane met a smooth-talking young man named Ray Bruné who would change everything, including her last name.

Who was this guy? I distinctly remember asking my father that question many years ago, and all I got in reply was a shrug of the shoulders and some dismissive language like, "I didn't know much about him, really." It's true that my father was living in New York by the time, and he probably wasn't being told anything about his older sister's life back in San Francisco. Even as a child, I could tell that what little he *did* know wasn't good, and he didn't want to talk about it.

So it fell to me and my beloved sister-in-law, Erika, to root out the story more than seventy years later. Like two dogs with a bone, Erika and I dove headlong into the Bruné family tree, spending long hours on the phone sharing discoveries. Erika even developed a spreadsheet to try to put together how the Tippett family and the Bruné family were connected. We were determined to bring a long-hidden family secret into the light. It took months but we finally put together the big picture, if not every single detail.

Herman Wideman Bruné, nicknamed Ray, was born into privilege in 1906, making him ten years younger than my Aunt Jane. His father, Alfred Ernest Bruné, was involved in San Francisco real estate, and his mother, Anna, was the daughter of a prominent German-born sugar baron in Honolulu who was very active in Hawaiian politics and was eventually appointed circuit court judge. Ray's grandmother was a native Hawaiian named Mary Kaumana Pilahiuilani Kapoli Kealaimoku. The Hawaiian roots of the family remained strong, and as a boy Ray traveled several times by steam ship with his family between San Francisco and Honolulu.

But all of that luster and privilege was abandoned by Ray when he was only eighteen and left his family home on Hyde Street to marry his girlfriend, Mary Frances Manning. A son, Robert, was born later that year. The marriage was very short-lived and in 1930, Mary Frances sued Ray for divorce, and she and the baby returned to Fresno to live with her parents. Ray took up residence in a San Francisco boarding house. It was in this boarding house that Ray met an Irish immigrant named James Carroll, who would soon play an important part in Ray's life. Now twenty-three, Ray was selling commercial stocks.

By 1933, Ray was living in Reno, Nevada, and opened a brokerage office called Raymond Lewis & Company. In an online newspaper search I did just a few years ago, I found a mention in the October 1, 1932, edition of the Reno newspaper's society column about an elegant bridal tea attended by 100 of Reno's "younger social set." And there, listed among the guests was a Jane Bruné. I was stunned. Had my Aunt Jane married this Ray Bruné and followed him to Reno? As much as I tried, I could not locate a marriage certificate for Jane and Ray in either state. Years later, a cousin on that side of the family speculated that they had run off to Mexico in the early 1930s and gotten married there, and then wished me good luck in finding any documentation to prove it. I had another theory: Maybe they never did get married and Jane just took his name to legitimize their relationship to their friends and families. I tried to imagine what Jane's relationship with the Bruné family could have been like. And did the Tippett family know about her relationship with Ray Bruné?

For all the questions the mere mention of Aunt Jane's name in the Reno paper had raised for me, this much was clear: Ray Bruné was indeed up to no good in Reno and it was public knowledge. According to records dug up by my sleuthing sister-in-law, Erika, by 1932 Ray had established a Nevada mining company called the Standard Pacific Development Company, naming himself as president and Jane Bruné as vice president and secretary. The company, which sold shares to investors, was soon deemed to be a sham. Soon thereafter, Ray Bruné and his accomplice and former San Francisco boarding housemate

James Carroll were indicted for similar offenses for selling stock in an asbestos mining company through another shell corporation, Raymond Lewis & Company.

According to the Reno Gazette, Raymond Bruné was tried in federal court in Carson City, Nevada, in January 1934 and found guilty along with four others, including James Carroll, of using the U.S. mails to defraud investors. Ray was sentenced to a six-year term in prison. His prison records are no longer available, nor are the trial transcripts. According to a prison archivist we consulted, Raymond W. Bruné, Inmate #386-TA, age twenty-seven, was sentenced in Carson City on February 5, 1934, and served one year at Federal Prison Camp #10 in Tucson, Arizona. How or why Jane Bruné was absolved of any guilt remains a mystery.

Jane, then thirty-seven, returned to San Francisco to live with her mother. To further complicate the matter, dear old Aunt Jane filled out a job application in December 1935 for a job as a stenographer in the U.S. Treasury Department, signing her name "Miss Jane Bruné, widow." She also made a slight adjustment to her age: claiming she was twelve years younger. Since she did not have an official birth certificate, I guess she knew the falsification would be impossible to trace. It worked. She got the job, so apparently her association with a convicted felon was not a deterrent to her working for the federal government. Ray's parents still lived in San Francisco, and I wonder how they felt about this new Bruné girl living in the same town. Or did they know each other and enjoy a friendship? I also wonder how much Jane told her own mother about her life in Reno with Ray Bruné.

When I was growing up, I remember Aunt Jane speaking very fondly of her sister, Anne's, only child, Eddie Westdorp. Eddie was clearly the apple of her eye. Many years later, when Eddie was an old man in a nursing home and Jane had been dead for several years, I asked Eddie about his relationship with Jane. His fondness for her was as deep as hers had always been for him. Today, as an adult who has much more knowledge of her, I wonder if Jane knew that Ray Bruné had a child. If indeed she married him, did she know that she had inherited a stepson? Did she have any relationship with little Robert Bruné who would have been a small child when Jane and Ray were together?

Aunt Jane eventually moved from the Treasury Department to work again at KSAN radio, and then filled in for six months at the medical office of her brother George, who was dying of lung cancer. She closed the books on his practice when he died in May 1941. Six months later, the United States entered World War II, and Jane got a job as a stenographer at the War Department in Fort Mason, reporting to Brig. Gen. Robert Wylie, who was in charge of preparing the port of San Francisco for wartime emergencies. Apparently, brigadier generals don't do background checks either.

She was transferred to Washington, D.C., to work in the Pentagon for the Department of the Army's transportation division, specializing in commercial and military air movements. By the time I was old enough to remember her visits to our family in New York, Aunt Jane had achieved a G-7 pay grade and held a security clearance. Apparently, the Pentagon ignores background checks too.

My enigmatic Aunt Jane Bruné, no longer Eva Tippett, stayed in classified government work until 1970 when she retired and returned to Newport Beach, California. By the time she died in 1992, Jane had taken another few years off her age and claimed she was born in 1912 instead of 1896. Apparently, the county of Los Angeles doesn't do fact-checking either.

Aunt Jane outlived her three siblings and died at the ripe old age of ninety-six (even though her death certificate said she was eighty). In her lifetime, she adjusted her birth date several times when it was convenient. She also jettisoned her given name Eva, opting for her middle name instead. But she hung fiercely on to her adopted name, Bruné, right up to the end. She also outlived Ray Bruné who wound up living alone in Room 309 of a hotel in downtown San Francisco. When he was found dead by the hotel manager, he was half in and half out of bed, partially dressed. There was "evidence of recent extremely heavy drinking," according to the coroner's report. He was fifty years old.

Through it all, Jane managed to drop a veil of silence over what was behind that name. With Ray Bruné's name plastered all over Nevada newspapers for two years, it's confounding to me why Jane wouldn't drop that name and return to her maiden name. But she didn't. Even after her death, no one in my family admitted they knew anything about Ray Bruné. It's impossible to believe that the downfall of a scion of a prominent San Francisco family wouldn't be talked about both inside the family and beyond. It took Jane's nephew's wife (Erika) and her niece (me), plus the miracle of the Internet, to find out who Ray Bruné was. And yet, there are still so many unanswered questions about him, about Jane, and what their real relationship was. Is it possible that my father knew every bit of this, and couldn't bring himself to talk about it because he was so ashamed? If so, he took Ray Bruné's story with him to the grave.

George William Tippett

One day I showed my father some illustrations of the heart and lungs I had done for my high school biology class, and after admiring my artwork, he said they made him think of his older brother, George, who had studied medical books filled with similar illustrations.

"Was your brother a doctor?" I asked, completely surprised. "Yes," was his reply. "He had an office in San Francisco. But he got sick and died." There was a pause. "That was before you were born," he added. And that's where the conversation stopped. Looking back, I should have pursued my line of questioning further, but I sensed my father was uncomfortable, so I remained quiet. If my father spoke little of his sister Jane, he said even less about his brother George. In our house, there was not one single photograph of George, not one mention of his birthday or date of death, or whether or not he had a family. It was as if he were invisible. Not only was he the uncle I never met, he was the uncle we never talked about. What was going on here? Was Uncle George yet another relative with a checkered past?

I couldn't answer those questions for many years. I regret not asking my father in his twilight years about George, in fact about everyone in his family. But years went by and it wasn't until I got hooked on genealogy that George's story began to take shape.

George William Tippett was born to George Henry Tippett and Corinda Lee Morrish in Grass Valley, California, in 1893. He was not their first born. Two sisters preceded him: Edith Tippett arrived in 1890, but only lived a month. She died of cholera. A funeral was held at home and her little casket was taken to the cemetery by a horse-drawn carriage. Two years later another little girl, Lenora, was born and she too died within a month and was also buried in the Grass Valley City Cemetery. Unfortunately, no headstones have survived to mark their graves; only their funeral records survive. My dad knew of these little girls, and insisted that Lenora's middle name was "Wyoming," supposedly given by her father who was working in the Wyoming mine in Grass Valley the day she was born. I was very disappointed that little Lenora's death records listed her name as only Lenora.

George was born, baptized and schooled in Grass Valley. Apparently, he never graduated from high school. By the time he was sixteen, he had left school and was working as a clerk in a drugstore. By then, the family had grown to include his sisters Jane and Anne, and a baby brother, my father James Russell. His income, however meager, must have been welcomed in this household, whose principal wage earner was a miner with unpredictable employment. When the family moved to Sacramento, George entered the pharmacy program at U.C. Berkeley, graduating in May 1915. He then joined his family in Sacramento and worked as a "druggist" in the Central Drug Store. By that time, he was twenty-three years old.

No sooner had George launched his career than the United States entered World War I on April 6, 1917. He registered for the draft two months later and five months after that, he was officially enlisted. He left his job as a pharmacist and was sent to Fort Riley, Kansas, to train for the Army's Medical Corps. After five months of training, Private First Class George W. Tippett (Service Number 934973) was assigned to the newly formed Emergency Hospital #7 and sent on a troop train to Camp Merritt in New Jersey to await shipment to France. Along the way, he began keeping a handwritten diary that chronicled his adventures as an Army medic for eight months, from April 28 to December 25, 1918.

To keep things in perspective, I would not be born for another twenty-five years and would not see his diary for more than sixty years after that. I am deeply grateful to the young woman who kept these pages for her mother, Mildred, the woman who married George many years after the end of the war. And to my sister-in-law Erika, family historian par excellence, who pursued that young woman, got her permission to copy them, and carefully delivered those precious pages to me.

For any family historian, original, eyewitness documents that describe events as they are happening is a treasure trove. Official documents like censuses, ship manifests, military draft cards or school transcripts are invaluable and attest to facts. But a first-person account is something altogether unique. So, to finally read his diary in his own handwriting was a thrill for me. I immediately fell down a rabbit hole that has held me in its thrall ever since. Clearly well-educated, George's spelling (even of the challenging names of French towns) and penmanship are impressive, especially by today's standards. He was obviously curious about everything around him. Even with sparse information about troop movements from his commanding officers, he figured out the details of where he was and where he was headed. He left no breadcrumbs of doubt about his assignment to care for the wounded and dying, or questions about his country's mission in a foreign land. To follow him closely for those eight months in 1918 was an opportunity to get into the mind of a very articulate and committed young man who thoroughly believed in his role as an American soldier fighting for the Allied cause against a common enemy.

From Camp Merritt, he was transported by train to the Hoboken, N.J., docks on the Hudson River, and on May 9, 1918, he boarded the military transport ship USS Pastores in a convoy of fourteen ships headed to Europe. The trip was unusually long and often tedious. They spent fourteen days at sea, experiencing fire drills in the middle of the night, target practice, and taking their battle stations over and over again. He reported seeing dolphins and shark fins that were initially thought to be enemy submarines, and the collective sigh of relief when they learned they were not German periscopes, but fish. He wrote on his tenth day at sea: "Called on deck at 3:00 A.M. and required to remain until after daybreak." No explanation was given for why they had to spend hours in the predawn dark; they just followed orders, day after day and night after night.

The troops were never told exactly where they were headed, and the men amused themselves trying to guess where they would land. Britain? France? Finally, land appeared on the horizon and on the morning of May 23, 1918, the Pastores anchored in Brest Harbor in the far northwest corner of Brittany, France. George described watching French fishing boats sailing in and out of the harbor: "The sails of these boats are very gorgeous." They remained for a week aboard the Pastores until the troops were ordered to march four kilometers to Camp Pontananezen, which he described as "seething with troops who came in for a day or two of rest." After several days, they were boarded into French box cars to begin an eleven-day ride to their first real assignment.

Their train headed southeast through Dijon and Tours, "traveling through a most beautiful country, similar to California, some parts like

Fairyland," he wrote. They arrived at Bourmont, "a very quaint old town with a very beautiful view of the upper valley of the Meuse from the ancient church." They busied themselves cleaning the hospital and listening to the battle stories of the "Tommies," as they called British soldiers. George noted, almost wistfully, that there was no sign of war where they were, and it was "far more peaceful than Kansas."

They finally arrived at Coulommiers, where they pitched tents and set up their mobile hospital. Patients arrived in trickles at first, then in waves. Many had been gassed and there were many German prisoners of war. Emergency Hospital #7 was ordered to move again, further east and closer to the action. George described the noise of increased fire by anti-aircraft guns trying to take down "Boches" (French for swine, a nickname for Germans, along with "Fritz," "Hun" and "Kraut," adopted by all Allied troops) planes headed to Paris. As patients arrived in waves, American planes overhead were flying bombing forays into German territory.

In mid-August, they struck their tents and supplies and moved the entire camp in 148 French trucks. They had seen 27,000 patients in two months. They moved to a spot near Verdun in "very pretty surroundings." A month later, the "Yanks" took back the occupied town of St. Michel, and German prisoners started arriving in droves. In a single day, they treated 1,053 patients. They were much closer to the Western Front by that time and George reported the sky was always lit up at night with anti-aircraft fire. On October 24, he wrote: "the most wonderful happening of the war" was to watch 350 American planes flying overhead on their way to the Argonne front, so thick "they blackened the afternoon sky like droves of blackbirds in a cornfield."

In early November, they received orders to move again, location unknown. They arrived at Saint-Juvin in the Meuse-Argonne region to the ghastly sight of thousands of dead bodies lying everywhere, wherever they fell. But there were hopeful rumors of an armistice. A few days later, on November 11, 1918, official news of the armistice reached their camp and celebratory bonfires and fireworks kept them awake all night.

The war was officially over, but they were on the move again, this time in American box cars to Verdun, where they followed the Moselle River, crossing into Germany. George reported that both sides of the river were filled with troops and trucks. On December 15, they arrived at Prüm, which he described as a "very nice town." They set up a hospital in the local high school, and by December 17 they were "open for business."

"December 25th: First Christmas in Europe. Nurses gave party in their recreation room to enlisted men." And that was George's last entry in his diary. I was devastated to read these last words. I wanted it to go on. I wanted to know about his time in Germany and what they did there for four months before his tour of duty ended. It's easy to imagine that his work continued without pause,

treating the wounded and dying from both sides: the gassed, the shell-shocked, the blinded, the amputees and the maimed.

I found documentation that he was finally shipped home from Brest, France, in April 1919, and disembarked at Boston before arriving back at Fort Riley, Kansas. The base staged a homecoming military parade for locals who celebrated their return from war. He was soon on his way home to Sacramento to live with his parents.

It was no surprise that George decided to go to medical school. After his experience in the military hospital, he was eminently qualified. It took him another twelve years to get his medical degree, but he had certainly found his calling.

According to the 1920 Census, one year after being discharged from the Army and at twenty-six-years-old, George was back in San Francisco living with his parents and siblings in an apartment on Bush Street. My father, the youngest child, was only eleven. George was once again working as a druggist. Although he was armed with a pharmacy degree from Berkeley, any dreams of moving on to medical school were thwarted by the fact that he had never gotten his high school degree. It must have both infuriated and humiliated George to do it, but in August 1920, he enrolled in Lowell High School, finished his last year of high school and graduated in June 1921. He wasted no time in matriculating at U.C. Berkeley's pre-med program and completed three years there before transferring to Stanford in 1923.

This photo of George was probably taken during his years in medical school.

For the next few years, the trail gets murky. George's father died in 1924 and it's possible George had to withdraw from school to help support his mother, then re-enter when he could afford the tuition. In 1926 he and his mother were living in Palo Alto while he attended classes at Stanford, and later worked as a technician at Lane Hospital. Finally, in June 1931, George got his medical degree from Stanford and was licensed to practice in the state of California. It had taken him twelve years from the date he was discharged from the Army to achieve his lifelong goal. He was thirty-seven-years-old. After so many years of shaping his future, George would have only a decade to enjoy the fruits of his labors.

Right away, George opened a medical office in the same office as Dr. Benjamin, the physician who had treated George's father prior to his death. He continued to live with his mother for the next several years until he met a young lady who turned his head.

Mildred Quinlan was thirteen years younger than George, and it was difficult for me to imagine how their paths could have crossed. He, a busy physician with a new practice, and she, a newly divorced bookkeeper. But they fell in love quickly and went to Reno to be married by a justice of the peace in February 1937. I found a copy of their marriage certificate listing the groom as George Tippett and the bride as Mildred Quinlan. But Quinlan wasn't her name, it was Bruné.

Mildred had been married to Ray Bruné's older brother, Alfred, at the time Ray was sentenced to prison. What's more, while out on bond, Ray Bruné gave my Uncle George's medical office address as a place where he could collect his mail and receive his personal belongings. My head was spinning as I connected the dots. My family's link to Ray Bruné's criminal life was not limited to my Aunt Jane, as I had always believed. My Uncle George not only knew Ray, he married Ray's former sister-in-law.

Erika and I returned to the stack of papers and mementos that she'd gotten from a Bruné relative the year before. We found a very poignant love note George had written to Mildred in 1937, two years after they met. In it, he mentioned an "illness" that brought them together. He also described "stormy times when life was very dark" for them. But their relationship endured through it all, and George ended the note by professing his "sincerest love" for Mildred. I have no way of knowing whose illness he was referring to, or even what storms he meant. I suspect some of that, though, had to do with Ray Bruné.

In fall 1940, George was diagnosed with lung disease and eight months later he died at the age of forty-seven. His mother buried him in San Francisco's Cypress Lawn Memorial Park in Colma next to his father. A decade later, his mother, Corinda, would be laid to rest there too. A fourth spot on the Tippett headstone was left blank, presumably for Mildred. It's still blank today.

Throughout my life, my father never once mentioned that his brother George had been married. I never once heard the name Mildred mentioned. It was as if a huge gulf existed between my father's life and the life of his family. Tracking

George and Mildred at home in San Francisco. Both George and Mildred were quite petite. According to his 1929 driver's license, George was only 5'6" tall, and Mildred looks to be about five feet tall.

back through the timeline of their lives as I constructed them on the website Ancestry.com, I could see that in the early 1930s the escapades of Jane and Ray, followed by the clear connection between George, Mildred and the Bruné family, coincided with the same time my father left California to go to New York to find work. It was the depths of the Great Depression, and he left on a gamble. He was only twenty-five, didn't know anybody in New York, had no work experience, and no guarantee of a job in New York. But I think my father was deliberately escaping the chaos and shame his family was living to seek a new life as far away as he could get.

George Henry Tippett and Corinda Lee Morrish

After exploring the lives of my father's brother and sister, I was naturally curious about the parents who raised them — the grandfather I never knew and the grandmother I barely remember. My grandfather died when my father was just a teenager, so even his memories were vague about a man who grew up in rural England and left that life behind to seek his fortune in America. I was so intrigued by the notion of this mysterious man, whom I considered an adventurer of great stature, that I couldn't wait to tuck into a research project on George Henry Tippett.

When I was a teenager, I asked my father one day about where his father had come from. "Lands End, in England," he replied. I had no idea where that was, so he explained it was the "boot" of southwest England that jutted into the Atlantic. "The county is Cornwall," he went on, "and their town was Redruth. Everyone was a miner in that part of England. My dad was a miner." And that was the end of my introduction to my English grandfather. It was going to take hours and hours of research on the Internet many, many years later for me to ferret out any further information about him.

George Henry Tippett was born at home in Cornwall, England, in the village of Illogan, just a mile or so from Redruth's town center in fall 1858. His parents were twenty-seven-year-old William Tippett, a copper miner, and his twenty-nine-year-old wife, Elizabeth Jane Pentecost Tippett. By the time he was ten, George Henry had seven siblings: two brothers and five sisters. For most of his youth, George Henry's father worked as a farmer, and it is certain that he helped in the fields from the time he was quite small. Indeed, in the 1871 Census, taken when he was thirteen, his occupation (he was no longer in school) was reported as "a farmer," helping his father farm twenty-five acres he didn't own. He was a tenant farmer.

So, what compelled George Henry to leave? What drives a person to uproot his whole life and set out for a foreign land to start all over again? I was absolutely intrigued by this question and dug into some books about the immigrant mindset. Social scientists point to what is called "push factors," those influences that convince an individual (or a family, or even groups of like-minded friends from the same community) to leave behind everything they know and embark on a life-changing journey to a new land. Epidemics of disease and famine are easily understood reasons to depart. So is intolerance – religious and political – and war. All of these are wrapped up in a pervasive fear that life at home will never improve and therefore a new life elsewhere would surely be better. Because George Henry was the second son born, it's tempting to conclude that the age-old practice of primogeniture played a part in his decision to leave. But that's not the case here. The Tippetts were not a wealthy bunch, and there was no fortune to inherit.

There were other influences on his decision, as well. Throughout his formative years, emigration from Cornwall to mines in Canada, Mexico, South Africa, Australia and America was occurring in huge numbers. The Cornish papers published weekly notices from major shipping lines, booking agents and lodging companies that offered their services to those making the trip. In the last months that George lived in Redruth in 1879, The West Briton newspaper repeatedly ran two columns of ads that made the prospect of such a long journey seem easy. Shipping agents in every corner of Cornwall, including an agent for the White Star Line with an office in Redruth, advertised their ships as having the best accommodations. Fairburn & Marrack in Liverpool offered to meet emigrants at the Liverpool train station and accommodate them in the Cornish House inn until their ship sailed. Across the pond, Mr. Alfred Williams, proprietor of the Miners' Arms on Front Street in New York, a well-known inn for Cornish miners, advertised that he was "always in attendance at the docks on arrival of all Liverpool steamers" and would also help the immigrant secure train passage to the mining areas of America. It is almost certain that George's journey was well planned in advance and that he utilized these services as he traveled.

It was 1879. The California Gold Rush had ended twenty years before, but the wave of migrants leaving Cornwall for America had continued unabated. Between 1825 and 1850, over a million British subjects left for the United States alone; many others emigrated to Australia, New Zealand and Canada. By 1879, when George left Cornwall, two-thirds of all of Cornwall's miners had emigrated to foreign countries. It is easy to imagine that almost everyone in Cornwall knew someone who had left for a chance at a better life.

To add to the gloomy picture, the Panic of 1873 had triggered a severe international economic recession in both Europe and the United States that would not release its grip. In the United States, the Bank of California had failed, and the "golden" state joined the depression. Mining operations in the Sierra foothills had fallen off significantly. Many of the original forty-niners were out of a job for the first time since they'd arrived.

But while the situation in California looked grim, it was worse in Cornwall. The Cornish mining industry was in sharp decline and a farming depression had begun. The Cornish had always been known as a people with few illusions, especially the miners who were accustomed to working under brutal conditions in the tin and copper mines, waiting patiently – often for years – before reaping any kind of payoff. Nonetheless, many figured that although working the mines in California would be just as grueling, the rewards for mining gold would be much greater. In spite of all the bad news, the allure of seemingly unlimited opportunity had not dissipated.

When George Henry left Cornwall, he was twenty years old and unmarried. Like his father, George had worked in the mines and also had farmed. Having attended school up to the age of thirteen, George could read and write, and as an able-bodied young man, he would have been an asset to any Cornish mining family. But they also knew that a portion of whatever he earned in America would be sent back home, income they sorely needed.

For miners from England determined to reach the "promised land" in California in the 1870s, the trip had become significantly easier than it had been for those who preceded them. Earlier emigrants had faced a two-week trans-Atlantic voyage to New York followed by another long sail south to the Isthmus of Panama where a train transferred them through the rainforest to the Pacific coast (no Panama Canal in those days). Another ship brought them north along the west coast of Mexico and California to San Francisco. For those headed to the mines of Grass Valley, a smaller boat steamed up San Francisco Bay to Sacramento where a stagecoach then took them the final fifty-seven miles to Grass Valley.

For George, the trip in 1879 was considerably shorter and easier. The transcontinental railroad linking New York to San Francisco had been completed in 1869, so the overland route – some 3,682 miles — had been reduced to four or five days, and cross-country travel had become almost commonplace.

On June 5, 1879, George boarded the Britannic, a 5,000-ton steamship that had been built by the White Star Line in Belfast, Ireland, only five years before. George was one of 766 passengers traveling in steerage, sharing cramped quarters with families with children, other single men, and starry-eyed couples. The ship made its way down the Mersey River from Liverpool to the Atlantic. The first stop was Queenstown, Ireland, some 250 miles across the Irish Sea where mail and additional emigrants were boarded for the transatlantic voyage. The ship arrived in New York Harbor eight days later on June 13, 1879. We Americans are steeped in the dramatic visual of the world's emigrants being buoyed by the breathtaking sight of Lady Liberty, that storied "Mother of Exiles" signaling the end of their long journey and welcoming "the tired, the poor and the huddled masses yearning to breathe free." But no, George Henry Tippett never saw this sight. The Statue of Liberty was not erected in New York harbor until 1886, seven years after he arrived.

His first glimpse of American soil was undoubtedly the Rotunda at Castle Garden at the tip of Manhattan, which was New York's only immigrant arrival depot from 1855 to 1890, processing over eight million new arrivals in those thirty-four years. He was just one of 179,589 arrivals in 1879, but was the first immigrant to the United States in my family.

My research could not tell me if George lingered or not in New York City, but whenever he headed to California, he undoubtedly got there by train. A well-developed network of regional trains weaved from New York through the eastern cities to Chicago across the farmlands of Iowa to Council Bluffs, Nebraska, near Omaha, which was the terminus of three Eastern railroads and where the Union Pacific Railway started its great western journey. The Union Pacific Railroad had established an Emigrant Waiting Room in Omaha as an accommodation for the hordes of emigrants settling in the West. An Eating Room sold dinners for 25 cents a plate and lodging could be had for the same price. Emigrant travelers could also purchase lunch baskets and other provisions for the long trip. The emigrant rate for the overland trip from New York to San Francisco was $65, not a trifling sum in those days, while first class passengers paid $138.35, a small fortune.

The train continued west to Reno, the last stop before reaching California. It was there that George disembarked to take the Virginia & Truckee line for the short twenty-five-mile trip to the Washoe mining region of Nevada. When he reached Virginia City, "Queen of the Comstock," George found a shanty town, a typical ramshackle mining camp. It could claim only one church but forty-seven gambling saloons, and there was no escape from the deafening noise of stamp mills and the pumps that were constantly pulling water from the mineshafts. And what were his employment prospects? What awaited him was the opportunity to join hundreds of other miners who were lowered every day by elevator cages as deep as 2,500 feet in some places into the sweltering underground heat. Thanks to the miners' union, the miners were mostly Cornish; no Irish or Chinese were allowed. The pay was about $4 for an eight-hour day, better than what he could earn in Cornwall.

The 1880 U.S. Census found George in southern Nevada in the Candelaria mining district in Esmeralda County, but he reported he had been out of work for six months. Candelaria didn't even have a name until 1865 but by the time George arrived in 1879, the Northern Belle Mine there was producing $33 million a year in silver. One year later, Candelaria had three doctors, three lawyers, two hotels, six stores, a post office, two newspapers, numerous saloons, a brothel, and not one single church. By 1882 George had moved further east and was in Ruby Hill, Nevada, which was a booming mining town in the center of the state with 2,500 residents, schools, churches, a theater and a brewery. It is fascinating for me to imagine this young chap from Cornwall with its fields of gorse and hedgerows, where any village is only a few miles from the sea, now living in the vast hot desert of the American West with its treeless, brown landscape, dry hills and not an ocean in sight. He must have loved the adventure of it all because he remained in the Nevada desert for three or four years, probably working in several different mines.

In a strange coincidence, Ruby Hill is about 165 miles from Tippett, Nevada, an old mining town named for John Tippett from Cornwall (no relation). It once had its own designated postal address but today is a ghost town, as is Ruby Hill. By 1885, the fortunes of Ruby Hill had declined and only 700 residents remained. But George had already left Nevada and had boarded the train again to finish the last leg of the journey that he started on the East Coast a few years before.

Five years after arriving in America, George was in Grass Valley, known as "The Quartz Crowned Empress of the Sierra," with a population of about 7,000 in the heart of Gold Rush country. He was not the first Cornishman to arrive in this little town. The Cornish had been brought to this area for their deep shaft mining expertise and by 1890 an estimated 60 percent of the population of Grass Valley was Cornish. George must have felt very much at home in the community of Cornish expatriates who called themselves "Cousin Jacks and Cousin Jennies." To the Americans, the Cornish were considered English, no different than a Londoner and even not much different than an Irishman. Ironically, the Cornish had never identified closely with Englishmen – they were Cornish first and English second — so the American attitude puzzled them. The flat, nasal American accent was peculiar to their Cornish ears so even communicating was, certainly at first, an effort. Back then, the town of Grass Valley was a haphazard collection of hastily constructed buildings of rough wood strung along dirt streets deeply rutted by wagon wheels. The main streets were covered in wooden planks, and residents were starting to see a few brick buildings going up. I wondered if a Cornish transplant like my grandfather missed the ancient villages of Cornwall with their whitewashed cob cottages connected by streets of cobblestone.

Many Cornish miners arrived in California never intending to stay. They went there determined to find gold, make money and return to Cornwall to live a comfortable life. Some set a time limit, giving themselves three, five or even ten years, after which they would go back to the tin mines of Cornwall, even if they were empty-handed, to pick up their lives where they left off. Only a few brought their families with them and spoke freely of settling down and into the American lifestyle. But for every Cornishman who bought shares in a California mine, built a house or married a local woman, the likelihood of returning home grew dimmer and dimmer. And if, after the requisite five years, a "Cousin Jack" filed a Declaration of Intent for American citizenship, he knew he'd never go back.

George stayed, and apparently made a decent living for himself.

In 1890, when he was thirty-one, George Henry Tippett married Corinda Lee Morrish, age twenty-three.

Corinda was the second of three daughters born to William and Catherine Lydia Williams Morrish, both of whom were immigrants from Cornwall. Like her sisters, Corinda had been born and raised in Grass Valley. Corinda's father, William, and George's father (also William) both died in 1889, so neither man was alive to see this

Taken in 1884 in Grass Valley, this photo shows George at age 26, looking the part of a successful man who has made his mark. He surely mailed this photograph to his parents to let them know that all was well with their son.

Corinda Lee Morrish

woman of Cornish parents marry this Cornish transplant. The wedding took place at the Morrish home in Grass Valley on New Year's Day 1890. Five months later, George became a naturalized citizen, swearing to renounce "all allegiance and fidelity" to Queen Victoria of England. Thus, George the Cornishman became a full-fledged American.

Just five years after getting married, George's adopted hometown had grown to sixteen grocery stores, ten barber shops, nine variety stores, seven clothing stores, five restaurants, four newspapers, three drug stores, two banks, and one store that sold pianos and organs. Leading all other retail establishments with forty-four locations was the liquor industry. The population had grown about 15 percent, to 8,000, in just five years.

There are no surviving records to reveal which mine employed George Henry Tippett during the years he lived in Grass Valley. However, I learned that the North Star mine hired mostly Irish workers, and that the Empire mine, by far the biggest and most profitable operation in the area, preferred to hire Cornish hard rock miners. A few years ago, I talked my son, daughter-in-law and two grandchildren into accompanying me on a trip to Grass Valley, where we toured the Empire Mine. My grandchildren were fascinated by the elegant home the mine's owner had built, especially the large kitchen with its "old-timey" utensils. It's not likely their great-great-grandfather ever set one foot inside that mansion, but even at their young ages, they could appreciate the difference in lifestyles between a mine owner and the dirty and dangerous work the miners did. A simulated trip down a mine shaft in a small cart, accented by the deafeningly loud clanging of warning bells and the roar of the high-speed descent was enough to convince them they didn't want to ever work as a miner.

Mining in those days was a weird business, cloaked in the promise of glamour but fraught with a messy reality. Many years later, my father would repeat a story he had heard his father tell many times:

As a youngster, my father was deep in a gold mine one day with an older man who was an expert at extracting the precious metal embedded in the rock. Holding a small lump of blackish rock in the palm of his hand, he asked my father, "What do you think this is?" The boy looked at it with a look of disgust on his face. "Why, that's just a piece of you-know-what from the outhouse," he replied. "Wrong!" said the old miner. "That's gold, son, and you gotta look carefully to find it, but it's there. And sometimes when you find it, you don't even recognize it." And sure enough, after scratching the rock with his fingernail, there it was: gold shining underneath the dirt and grime.

Was it a true story? Does it matter?

After thirty years in Grass Valley, George moved, alone, 115 miles east across the Sierra Nevada to Virginia City, Nevada, to work in the mines there, where it all started for him. It was 1910, and there were barely 3,000 people living in all of Storey County, and Virginia City claimed 75 percent of them, less than a quarter of the number of people who had lived there during the boom days when George passed through as a new immigrant in 1879. Men still outnumbered women two to one, and the desert climate was hotter in the summer and colder in the winter than they were used to in Grass Valley. Perhaps it was his last attempt, at age fifty-one, to find success as a miner.

It was short-lived. A few years later, the family relocated to Sacramento. He was fifty-six by that time, and perhaps no longer able to withstand the physical demands of mining. Corinda's sister Anne, who had also married a Cornishman, lived there with their three grown children, so they had family there. Still, George and Corinda lived at no less than three different addresses, and he changed jobs frequently. He finally found work in the "shops" of the Southern Pacific Railroad, the largest industrial complex west of St. Louis. He did maintenance and repairs on freight cars, earning about 40 cents an hour. I discovered his old pay stubs online and was shocked to see that his bi-weekly paycheck averaged about $50. Ever the patriot, he occasionally had $12 taken out of his paycheck in order to buy a World War I savings bond.

In what would be the last move of his life, George and his family moved to San Francisco where he found temporary work as a cabinetmaker. A large family of six, they lived together in an apartment of about 1,100 square feet. Five years later, ill and unable to work, George died at home in 1924 at the age of sixty-five. The cause of death was chronic myocarditis and bronchial asthma, conditions that plagued those men who spent too many days underground in dank, stifling mines.

The legacy he left was certainly not one of wealth and riches, but one of self-sufficiency and hard work. My father, who was only sixteen at the time, inherited those qualities in full measure. Good Cornish genes? American grit? Blue-collar determination? Pride in hard work? Unshakeable ambition? Absolutely.

WILLIAM MORRISH AND CATHERINE LYDIA WILLIAMS

On a sunny fall weekend at my son Eric's house in Santa Cruz, the family gathered for an important project. My brother, Jamie, and his wife, Erika, (who shares the genealogy gene with me), my son Eric and his wife, Carmen, and I were there on a missing person's assignment. Erika had lugged the box crammed with old photos salvaged from my mother's garden shed, and our job was to identify, once and for all, the tintype of that scary lady dressed in black with the blazing eyes and tight mouth. Stuck on the back of the tintype was our only clue: On an old mailing label someone had written "Grandmother Morrish." Okay, we agreed, that definitely put her on our father's maternal side of the family, but who was she? We laid out all the old photos in a family tree pattern to see where the missing piece was. After a great deal of deliberation, we decided this wretched-looking woman was none other than Catherine Lydia Morrish, the mother of my grandmother Corinda Lee Morrish.

Erika and I soon embarked on a deep dive into Ancestry.com to find out more about this fearsome lady. She was born Catherine Lydia Williams in Kea, Cornwall, in 1834, and was

Catherine Lydia Williams

baptized in the Bible Christian Church. Her father was a copper dresser who pounded rocks to release the embedded copper metal in the Twelve Heads mining district, near the towns of Redruth and Truro. When she reached the age of twenty-one in 1855, she married twenty-six-year-old William Morrish from nearby Bizza Pool. Shortly thereafter, William sailed to New York to find mining work in the American West, and she followed a year later. At the time of her sailing in June 1866, she was traveling with a one-year-old daughter, Anne Marie, and was almost eight months pregnant with my grandmother Corinda, who was born just a few weeks later in Grass Valley.

Plunging right into their new American life, her husband, William, took out naturalization papers, and in fall 1868, William was "admitted to citizenship" in the United States in a group ceremony that included men from Ireland, Scotland, Wales, England, Portugal, France and Italy. Catherine took no such action. She didn't have to. At that time, women were mere appendages of their husbands, so if the husband became a U.S. citizen, so did she.

William worked as a miner, but he also created a massive garden in Grass Valley's Boston Ravine. At an elevation of 2,500 feet, the area was warm enough for growing vegetables and cool enough for fruit trees, so William planted row crops and fruit trees. The garden was soon providing enough income to supplement his mining wages. A third daughter, Edith, was born in 1869. Eventually, William's brother Thomas joined the family and helped with the gardening. From time to time William returned to the mines, but continued to work his large garden, which had become quite well known for bountiful harvests of perfect fruit.

Family lore claims that the highly prized produce and fruit from William's garden was sold as far away as San Francisco and that it was delivered by none other than George Henry Tippett, who would one day marry the Morrish daughter, Corinda. While it's true that George Tippett lived in Grass Valley at the time and did in fact marry Corinda in 1890, the great distance from Grass Valley to San Francisco (more than 150 miles) in a horse-drawn wagon or on the narrow-gauge railroad while keeping produce cool and fresh makes this story highly improbable. But it's possible, I suppose. We have no way of knowing.

During spring 1889, William's beautiful garden was being ravaged by a wild boar that was destroying the plants. William spent several nights driving the animal off, but the beast eventually attacked and gored him in the leg. It got badly infected, but William refused his doctor's advice to amputate the limb, and several weeks later, on May 25, 1889, he died of blood poisoning. His family held his funeral at their home on South Auburn Street not far from the garden. A horse-drawn hearse followed by two carriages for the family led from the home to the Methodist Episcopal Church for a memorial service. He was buried in the Grass Valley Public Cemetery the same day.

As I sat in the Grass Valley Historical Society on a rainy winter afternoon reading this story from the May 25, 1889, edition of the Grass Valley Daily Union, I couldn't believe the words on the page. Gored by a wild boar? I was incredulous. The whole thing was positively medieval. Even in the late nineteenth century, who got attacked by a boar? And who died from the wounds? I was so stunned that I shared it with the librarian who had set up the microfiche for me. Her eyes landed on the sentence, "He would not consent to amputation until it was too late." But the librarian wasn't surprised, only bemused. "Typical Cornishman," she said. "Stubborn beyond all reason."

Because the incorrigible William Morrish died without a will, his estate entered into probate in Nevada County Superior Court. Catherine, a widow in her mid-fifties who couldn't read or write, named her eldest daughter, Annie, as administrator of the estate. The estate included the Morrish Gardens, their homestead, four lots sandwiched in between the North Star Mines and the vast Empire Mines, plus water rights to several ditches, a water flume and an access road — land that the Empire Mine would have loved to acquire. Because women could not own property in their own names, Catherine had to first petition the court to establish her rights to the property. For ten years, the Empire Mine fought for, and finally won, the land and water it wanted. I couldn't find any documents that showed my great-grandmother benefited financially from these transactions. I think the powerful mine owners and their legal teams took advantage of a poor, illiterate woman and paid her a pittance, if anything at all, to fatten their portfolios.

Sadly, the Morrish Gardens were eventually sold off. Catherine continued to live alone, even after her three daughters and all thirteen of her grandchildren moved to Sacramento. By the time she reached age eighty, she had fallen ill with a heart condition. In the winter months of 1915, her daughters Annie and Edith came to her home on Race Street in Grass Valley to care for her.

When she died on February 9, the front page of The Grass Valley Union newspaper ran a column about her, saying:

For forty-four years she made her home at the celebrated Morrish gardens on South Auburn Street... Had Mrs. Morrish lived until the day set for her funeral, she would have been 84 years of age.

The newspaper got her age wrong, probably because her daughters reported it incorrectly. Still, the size of the headline "FUNERAL OF MRS MORRISH THURSDAY" was a sign of the respect she enjoyed in her American hometown. The funeral, held in her home, was well attended and she was buried the next day in the Grass Valley City Cemetery on February 11, 1916.

I found myself trying to reconcile the ferocious face on that old tintype to the obvious affection my great-grandmother enjoyed in Grass Valley. Thanks to the Internet, I located an historian in England who specialized in women's and men's fashions. I emailed her a copy of the old photo, and she had this to say:

"Tintypes were very popular in the United States starting in the mid-1850s. In this image, Catherine is wearing good daytime clothing over a white blouse whose cuffs are visible at her wrists. The narrow bands of black trim around her cuffs and shoulders are typical decorative details of the late 1860s and early 1870s. The distinctive white collar, or jabot, crossed over her chest in front would indicate this photo was taken in the 1870s."

By then Catherine was living in Grass Valley and would have been in her late thirties or early forties. It's possible this photo was taken in 1874 to mark her fortieth birthday. Although the subjects in almost all early photographs sat unsmiling, staring directly into the camera – an appearance which, to contemporary eyes, makes them all seem menacing at worst and glum at best — a smile or grin would have been considered inappropriate to our ancestors (who also usually had less than perfect teeth). Instead, they sought to project a demeanor of serious thoughtfulness.

Maybe I had been too judgmental about this woman who looked like a dragon lady but wasn't fierce enough, or educated enough, to stand up to the mining magnates who ran those massive operations right next door. I started to feel sorry for her. And found myself profoundly admiring of this tiny woman who held her own, until she could no longer.

Several years ago, my son, his family and I drove around South Grass Valley where the famous Morrish Gardens had once flourished. The countryside there is still beautiful, but we could find no evidence of an orchard or of tilled earth where rows of vegetables had grown. We did spy two gnarly old pear trees along a dilapidated fence, which was all the proof we needed that we had found the right spot. The mines had been silenced for many years, so there was no noise to disturb the tranquility of the place. Still, we felt a great longing for what had once thrived there.

And a deep resentment for the land grab that had deprived Catherine and William's heirs of their right to enjoy it how it had once been.

Isaac Williams and Catherine Ley

There was one more treasure in that box of photos found in my parents' garden shed that I just couldn't ignore. It was a beautiful sepia photograph of an old woman dressed in a long black skirt covered by an oversized jacket, a prim silk cap tied tightly under her chin, and holding a closed umbrella. Neither my sister nor brother nor I had any idea who she was, but there was something about her face that reminded me of my grandmother Corinda Morrish Tippett at the same age.

Fortunately, there was a handwritten note on the back that said: "Great Grandma Williams, Preacher in Church, age about 75 years, taken in England in 1874. Grandma Morrish's mother." It would be many months later, after extending my paternal family tree quite a bit more, that I was able to determine that this woman was Catherine Ley Williams, my second great-grandmother. That discovery was eye-popping enough, but a preacher?

Not too long afterward I became a member of the Cornwall Family History Society, which opened up new avenues of research gold to me.

Catherine Ley

The staff there was remarkably helpful whenever I submitted a request for information. I began to wait on my front porch in Ojai for the mail to arrive whenever I expected records about my English ancestors, and the sight of an oversized envelope with the imprint of the Crown on it sent my spirits soaring.

With CFHS help, I decided to reach back one more generation beyond Catherine and William Morrish and see what I could find. I was becoming aware that the further back family historians reach, the less information is available. Fewer and fewer people could read or write, so gems like diaries are practically nonexistent. Handwritten parish records have been digitized by the millions, unless they were lost to fire, which happened all too often. Birth, marriage and death certificates are held by the GRO, the General Records Office, and regional historical societies work heroically to preserve as many maps and newspapers as they can. And I could never forget the epic work done for generations of Mormons, who research and make available reams and reams of records. Armed with all this expertise at my disposal, I hoped to discover more about Catherine Williams' parents, my great-great-grandparents.

Tapping into several sources, I found out that Isaac Williams was baptized on February 12, 1807, so he was probably born late in 1806. His parents were John Williams and Lydia Chegwin, who lived in Kea, a mining town less than five miles east of Redruth in Cornwall.

His wife Catherine Ley, known as Kitty, was born to John Ley and Elizabeth Johns on April 11, 1811, in the town of Penryn, a nearby granite mining area. Two months after her birth, her parents baptized her into a Methodist denomination called the Bible Christians. This would turn out to be immensely important to how she lived her adult life.

On Sunday afternoon of June 2, 1833, Catherine and Isaac married. He was twenty-six and she was twenty-two. Within the first eight years of their marriage, she gave birth to six children. Although I was shocked by this fact, I had to remind myself that having so many children was common in the nineteenth century. Women usually found themselves pregnant every other year, despite how arduous and risky childbirth was in those days.

Doctors at that time did not deliver babies; childbirth was the domain of women, and even husbands were usually not present at a birth. Women gave birth at home and were attended by the mother's female friends and family members. Sanitation was primitive by modern standards. Pain relief was minimal and limited to encouraging the woman to pull against bed linens during contractions. Herbal teas were probably administered for calming. And the period of postpartum rest and recovery was undoubtedly short, as women of the lower classes did not have the luxury of servants to take over the household tasks. I imagine neighbors and siblings pitched in to help out while the new mother regained her strength.

England's Census of 1841 reported that Isaac and Catherine and their six children were living in Twelveheads, a tiny village between Truro and Redruth. Isaac worked as a copper dresser, not down in the mines, but doing manual labor "on the surface" separating copper from the rock in which it was embedded. Even though he was still a very young man in his thirties, he was seriously ill with consumption. I suspect that after years of working underground in the damp, foul air of a mine, he had been re-assigned to work above ground to ease his condition.

But it was too late. Just eight weeks after the Census was taken, Isaac died. He was only thirty-four and left a young family of six children and his thirty-year-old widow to fend for themselves.

Catherine continued to live in Twelveheads and a decade later, in 1851, she, a forty-year-old widow with three children still living at home, was working as a "plain worker" doing simple sewing and needlework. Her fourteen-year-old daughter, Elizabeth, was working as a "mine girl," doing manual labor breaking up the ore brought to the surface for dressing. Curiously, Catherine's eldest child, a daughter also named Catherine who was seventeen at that time and would become my great-grandmother, could not be found anywhere on the 1851 Census. The experts at the Cornwall Historical Society suggested she may have been living with another family in the area, doing domestic work to earn wages.

About this same time, a charismatic Methodist preacher was becoming very well known in this part of Cornwall. Twelveheads was the birthplace of William Trewartha Bray, known locally as Billy Bray. His father and grandfather had been pious Methodists, although Billy himself, a hard-drinking tin miner, lived a degenerate life. There were many stories about how his wife had to drag him home from the pub each night to try to sober him up. After a horrendous accident in the mine that almost killed him in 1823, he changed his life and joined the Methodist Bible Christians and became an evangelist to his former brethren in the mines. He became known for his preaching style, which encouraged raucous singing, jumping and shouting, all "to the glory of God." He died in 1868 after amassing a large following and building three chapels in the area.

A major tenet of the Bible Christian church (into which Catherine had been baptized) was the extensive use of women as ministers. They served as "local preachers" who worked part-time in their communities "abounding in the work of the Lord." These women were faithful followers of the Biblical injunctions to feed the hungry, clothe the naked, attend to the sick and visit those in prison. Methodism was popular among the poor working classes in the mining villages, and for those women who were intelligent but lacked any formal schooling, being trained as a lay preacher was a way to assume a leadership role, learn public speaking, and enjoy the respect of their neighbors.

I studied that old photo carefully and started to connect the dots. I am quite certain Catherine had become a lay preacher in the Bible Christian Church, and thus her later life started to make sense to me.

By the time the 1861 British Census was taken, Catherine was fifty and living in the Truro Union Workhouse, working as a nurse for the indigent residents. This fact opened up a new area of research for me. Workhouses today, I hope, are a thing of the past, but in the nineteenth century, they were England's way of dealing with the poor who ranged in age from infants to the elderly of both sexes.

The workhouses were large stone facilities with ample land for pigs and horses, and fields for growing crops. A master and matron were in charge of the daily schedule and were assisted by a schoolmaster and mistress. Each workhouse had an infirmary that employed one nurse (who had no formal medical training) to look after seventy-five to eighty beds with some help from able-bodied inmates. New arrivals were stripped and bathed with soap and water and issued a uniform. The bathing of inmates followed a very strict set of rules. The water temperature, regulated by a thermometer, was to be no cooler than 90 degrees and no warmer than 98 degrees. Bathing more than one patient at a time was prohibited. Under no circumstances was a patient's head to be put under water. Upon leaving the tub, the paid staff member made sure the patient was thoroughly dried and re-clothed.

After the bath, their old clothes were boiled and disinfected and returned to their owners only when – and if — they left the workhouse. Families were split up, as men, women and children were assigned separate quarters. The narrow beds had straw mattresses. The infirmary had only one bathroom and hot water was hand-carried from the laundry room. Meals were served in a common dining hall and were meager; only on Christmas Day did the inmates enjoy roast beef, plum pudding and cake that was donated by the community.

A job advertisement posted in 1873 reveals this about nursing in a Cornish workhouse: Her duties were to attend the sick and lying-in (maternity) wards, administer medications under the direction of the medical officer, and to see that a light was kept on at night in the sick ward. Only women who were widowed or single, and between the ages of twenty-five and forty, were eligible for hiring. The salary that was offered was £20 a year and included lodging and the usual rations in the workhouse. A nurse needed to be able to read a doctor's simple directions. This then, was the way my great-great-grandmother supported herself and lived out her faith.

In 1871, she was sixty years old and working as a nurse for the 124 inmates at the St. Clement Union Workhouse (the new name for the original Truro Union Workhouse). On August 3, 1873, the Royal Cornwall Gazette published an article describing an assault on Catherine by one of the inmates. The man, who was blind, had been using "bad language" and was admonished by Catherine so he struck her three times. He was arrested and sent to prison for fourteen days of hard labor.

Undaunted, Catherine forged on to answer her calling. The 1881 Census reports that Catherine, now in her mid-sixties, was a live-in nurse at 66 Fairmantle Street in Truro, the home of two elderly widows, Honor Johns and her blind sister, Eliza Hore.

Ten years later, Catherine, eighty years old and probably showing signs of dementia, had made the long trip "upcountry" to the northern county of Lancashire to live with her second-oldest daughter, Elizabeth Ann. (Catherine Lydia, my great-grandmother, had already immigrated to California.) The household in Burnley, Lancashire County, consisted of her daughter's husband, Joseph Thomas, who was a fifty-five-year-old coal miner, my great-aunt Elizabeth Ann, also fifty-five, their son James, a thirty-one-year-old cotton weaver, and their daughter, Catherine, a twenty-five-year-old cotton weaver. In the Census, my great-great-grandmother Catherine described herself as a retired nurse.

Catherine died in Burnley (where that photograph had been taken about six years before, possibly to commemorate her eightieth birthday) in June 1897. She was eighty-six years old. Her daughter Elizabeth Ann stated on the death certificate that her mother had died of "senile decay." She was buried on June 24 in the Thomas family's plot in the Burnley Cemetery, where her daughter's husband, Joseph, would be laid to rest just six months later.

At this point, I could look at my family tree that reached back four generations. Catherine Ley Williams was the one of my eight great-great-grandparents on the Tippett side of the family that I admired the most. All eight had been born in Cornwall and lived their entire lives in England. None of them emigrated to America for a "new beginning." They toiled to eke out a living. I was humbled by how, in spite of immeasurable hardships common in their lifetimes but unknown to us in the twenty-first century, they endured.

Catherine Ley Williams lived a very long life even by today's standards, but especially for a nineteenth-century woman. She lived through the reigns of four British monarchs. She witnessed the inventions of the light bulb, the telephone, telegraph, typewriter and the sewing machine. It was an era of huge advances in rail transportation and global steamship travel. Because of her work as a lay nurse, she surely knew of the discovery of the stethoscope, anesthesia, X-rays, pasteurization for milk, the introduction of germ theory, and news about the first vaccines for cholera, anthrax, rabies, tetanus, diphtheria, typhoid fever and the plague.

In her own right, Catherine lived a remarkable life of service, dedicated to the poor, the infirm and the needy. She survived her husband by fifty-six years, raising their children on her own, then working for almost fifty years as a nurse. Undoubtedly this commitment was driven by her religious faith that called her to do "the Lord's work" by caring for others and spreading her version of Christianity to those in her care. She may have been my first ancestor to achieve a profession, and although she was undoubtedly paid a mere pittance for her work as a nurse and caretaker, she has become a surprising role model for me for having been a strong, resilient and independent woman.

WILLIAM TIPPETT AND ELIZABETH JANE PENTECOST

After making some good progress on my family tree, I was anxious to share my discoveries with my brother, especially the new stuff on the Tippett side of the family. He took my printout of the family tree, studied it for a minute or two, then shrieked, "Pentecost! I never once heard that name mentioned, ever!" He shot an accusing glare at me and went on: "Don't you think we'd have heard that name at some point?"

"Yes," I conceded, "but not ever hearing it doesn't make it a mistake. Besides, I have documents to prove that our great-grandmother was Elizabeth Jane Pentecost, born in 1831 in Cornwall. And she married William Tippett and produced our grandfather George Henry Tippett. It's true."

Out came the documents. William Tippett was born in 1831, but because birth certificates were not required in England until 1837, his exact date of birth is not known. The parish priest entered, "William, son of William, a miner, and Sarah," into the parish record book when he was baptized in St. Euny, Redruth's parish church, by Rev. Hender Molesworth. I immediately fell in love with that pastor's name, which sounded so

Dickensian. I pictured this man of the cloth as a tall, hooked-nosed busybody who lurked around the church grounds in a black cassock and scared small children. Alas, he lived before photography was invented, so I'll never know if my guess is accurate.

William was born into a mining family in Redruth, a town that was the center of the mining industry for Great Britain. At that time, Redruth, with just over 8,000 inhabitants, was considered to be a large town. By the 1840s, there were some 112 copper mines in Cornwall employing about 60,000 people, and the tin mines employed about 12,000 more. Redruth was the richest metal mining area in Britain; indeed, Cornish tin dominated the world market until the 1870s, the peak of production.

Mining was a dangerous job, and life for mineworkers was mostly one of hardship and poverty. Walking through all sorts of weather, sometimes several miles from their cottages in their everyday clothes, they went first to the engine house where they changed into their underground work clothes, a simple suit of cloth pants, jacket and hat. Then they climbed into a mere hole in the ground and descended wooden ladders to their assigned level where they worked in pairs, usually brothers or fathers and sons. A hundred feet below ground, it was extremely hot and humid. The air was full of dust and rock particles. There were no hard hats to protect their heads from falling rock or timbers; instead, miners wore their own cloth or felt hats with a metal plate mounted with clay on the front that held a candle – their only light in the pitch-black darkness. Small boys pushed wheelbarrows filled with ore to the perpendicular shaft where it was hoisted in buckets "to grass" where surface laborers hammered it into smaller pieces. Large-scale disasters in the mines occurred often, killing dozens at a time. Death and injury from explosions and accidental falling were an everyday fact of life.

Miners worked for six to eight hours at a time six days a week. At that time, men working down in the mines earned up to £3 a month (equivalent to about $220 in 2010), while surface laborers made around £2 a month. Boys working below or above ground earned less than a pound a month and girls working above ground as "bal maidens" – those who used hammers to break up the ore into smaller pieces that could be crushed into coarse gravel – made only 15 to 18 shillings a month.

In spite of their tight bodices and sleeves, they worked on the ore that was brought up in large buckets from deep in the mine, using hammers to smash the ore into small chunks to reveal the metal. Their white bonnets and aprons were considered "protective" clothing. Note the size of the shovels they used to shovel the large pieces onto a hammering table. It was dirty, dusty work.

Most mining families lived in small, rented whitewashed cottages scattered around the general area of the mine in which they toiled with a few

These bal maidens (Cornish "bal" for mine, and English "maidens" for girls) were photographed at a mine in Cornwall in 1890.

acres of land to tend, or in row terraces of granite cottages with small courtyard gardens. There was no electricity or running water in their homes. The toilet was outside. A fireplace provided their only source of heat by burning furze, a scrubby plant gathered by hand, most trees having been felled for use in the mines. Parents and children slept on straw mattresses, usually several children sharing a bed. The women cooked on a wood fire. A typical meal was hot tea, potatoes, and occasionally salted pilchards, small herring-like fish netted in vast schools by local fishermen in the fall and winter.

In town, while amenities like gas lighting and a railroad station were established in Redruth by the 1830s when William was born, clean water and sewers weren't installed until the 1880s when he was a grown man in his fifties. Water was obtained from twenty-four taps, located in various parts of town. The supply was unreliable; most of the area's water was drained off by the vast mining operations.

By the time he was ten, William had five sisters. His father was a miner, and the family lived in a neighborhood called Forge in Redruth. In the first decade of his life, William and his siblings survived a typhus epidemic that swept through Britain from 1831 to 1834, followed by measles, smallpox and cholera outbreaks that claimed the lives of thousands of children, especially in the bigger cities like London.

On October 23, 1856, when he was twenty-five, William – who was then farming full time –

married Elizabeth Jane Pentecost, a woman from the village of Ruan Minor on the Lizard peninsula on the south coast of Cornwall. I had the chance several years ago to visit Ruan Minor, and it is an enchanting spot. Quiet, bucolic, and lush with trees and lawns, I could have happily moved to Ruan Minor to spend my days strolling down its lanes lined with little cottages and walled gardens.

Elizabeth was the daughter of Simon Pentecost, a shoemaker, and his wife, Eliza, who had moved their family up to Redruth a few years before. Elizabeth Jane was described in the marriage records as a twenty-seven-year-old "spinster," meaning she had not been previously married. They married in St. Euny Church where William had been baptized as a baby. With five sisters, William undoubtedly inherited many responsibilities early in his life. His father was a copper miner, and although copper mining was thriving and work was plentiful, the family's lifestyle was modest at best. No one in the family could read or write, so manual labor was their only choice. There were no child labor laws in force at that time, so William probably started working at a mine by the time he was eight or nine years old.

In the first four and a half years of marriage, Elizabeth and William had four children. According to the 1861 Census their children were: William John, my grandfather George Henry, Thomas, and a two-week-old daughter, Laura Emma. Also living with them was Elizabeth Jane's mother, Eliza Pentecost, a fifty-eight-year-old widow. William, then thirty years old, was farming twelve acres of land in Illogan, just outside of Redruth, and employed one boy to help with the farm.

By that time, Redruth had swelled to a population of more than 11,000 people and boasted three commercial banks, three foundries, a miners' infirmary, and four first-class hotels. By spring 1878, the Great Western Railway ran from London all the way to Penzance and was outfitted with sleeping cars; Redruth was firmly connected to the rest of the country. Tiny Illogan was home to 9,000 residents, twenty working mines, four post offices and eighteen churches. The area was thriving, and William's family lived in the heart of it.

A decade later, in 1871, William and Elizabeth Jane were living on the Nancekuke Road in Redruth with eight children: three boys and five girls, ages thirteen to four. Four daughters had been born since the last Census in 1861: Elizabeth Jane, named after her mother and called Lilly, Elizabeth Ann (called Annie), Mary Ellen (called Nellie) and Ada. William was a farmer of twenty-five acres.

In a family portrait, William is seated in the center with his wife, Elizabeth Jane, who is holding the family bible. Behind them stand Annie, John, Lillie, Laura, George Henry (my grandfather), and Tom. George Henry, who was twelve and a half, had left his school days behind and was working with his father and older brother

A family portrait taken about this time (1873-74) shows a well-dressed family in their "Sunday best," (dresses, suits with vests, leather shoes) with the family dog, Keeper.

as a farmer. Nellie and Ada are seated on the floor with Keeper, the family dog.

According to my fashion historian in England, the composition is typical of Victorian photographs with the parents seated together in the center, the youngest children seated at their feet, and the older, taller children surrounding them symmetrically in the back. Elizabeth Jane is dressed in a conservative day dress of colored fabric accented by dark trim, and wears a narrow day cap, typical for married women of this era. William is wearing a three-piece business suit and a bow tie that was popular in the 1850s and

1860s. The tie is a bit on the old-fashioned side, as is his beard, which was outmoded by 1870. He also sports a watch on a chain, something that was treasured by men throughout their lives. Since most formal portraits at this time were made to celebrate a milestone, it's possible this photograph was taken in 1871 to mark William's fortieth birthday, or the couple's fifteenth wedding anniversary.

A few years later, in 1881, the family was living at 7 Penryn Street in downtown Redruth, just steps from the wooden viaduct of the Great Western Railway. It could not have been a pleasant location, what with the noise of the train and the shaking timbers. The Census taken that year reports William was working as a tin miner and Elizabeth Jane was a grocer. Thomas assisted in the shop, and Lilly and Annie had jobs in the town while Nellie and Ada were presumably in school. My grandfather, George Henry (age twenty-two), had already immigrated to America, and his older brother, William John, had gone to Australia. They each may have been sending money home from time to time, something most Cornish miners living abroad did, but there are no records of this. The family income was supplemented by rent from five boarders, a very typical practice in Cornwall where more than half of all lodgers working as miners lived in the homes of fellow miners.

William died at the age of fifty-seven on February 20, 1889. His death certificate described him as a farmer who lived on Dopps Row in

Redruth. Other records list him as a driver of horse wagons. His youngest daughter, Ada, was present at his death, which was caused by bronchitis, a common affliction for miners whose lives were typically shortened by lung diseases. He was buried in what is now called the Redruth Municipal Cemetery on the Redruth-St. Day Road. I visited those burial grounds on my trip to Cornwall a while back, and the cemetery is what the British call "derelict" – the grounds are not maintained, the chapel is all but collapsed, and many headstones have toppled to the ground and broken. The weeds were knee-high. Pigeons flew in and out of wide gaps in the rotten roof. There is no marker for William, but municipal records identified his plot as A-339.

William's widow remained in Redruth, moving to a terrace house at 58 East End. Thomas, Annie and Ada, now in their mid- to late-twenties, were all unmarried and shared the house with her along with their married sister, Nellie, two grandchildren and two lodgers. By the spring of 1901, Elizabeth, then seventy, and Annie (a thirty-four-year-old draper's assistant) were living at 33 East End with grandson Harry Goad (then seventeen) and two lodgers.

This photo portrait is called a vignette, a style where the head and shoulders of the subject fades around the edges into a blank background. Elizabeth is wearing a dressy bodice ornamented with shiny black glass beads that fastens down the front with small buttons for a close fit and is anchored by a narrow bar brooch typical of

Elizabeth Jane Pentecost Tippett

the 1890s and early 1900s. Her puffed sleeves, called gigot or leg-o-mutton, were very popular in the 1890s. Her ornate white day cap trimmed with lace is a traditional accessory worn by older women whether married, single or widowed. At this time, Elizabeth would have been about seventy years old, so it is likely she dyed her hair to hide the grey, a common practice among elderly women. It is also likely the photographer retouched the image to hide wrinkles in her face. It is possible this photograph was taken in 1904 to mark her seventieth birthday and may be the last photograph of her taken in Cornwall before she immigrated to Western Australia in 1908.

In July 1908, at age seventy-nine, Elizabeth Jane and Annie (then forty-one) boarded a Royal Mail ship at Plymouth, England, and sailed to Perth, Australia, to join Annie's sister Lilly, who lived there with her husband. Annie died of typhoid fever six months after their arrival. Elizabeth Jane died eighteen months after her daughter from a cerebral hemorrhage. She was buried next to her daughter on February 13, 1911, in the Wesleyan section of Karrakatta Cemetery, a few miles from 17 Lacey Street in Perth, where they lived with Lilly and David Williams. Her death record states that she was survived by two sons – George Henry (my grandfather who was living in Virginia City, Nevada, at the time) and Thomas – plus three daughters: Elizabeth Jane "Lilly," Nellie and Ada. Her first son, William John, had died in Victoria, Australia, in 1905, where he worked as a miner.

The family that had for so many generations been firmly rooted in Redruth became the first generation of Tippetts who ventured abroad to live. The oldest son, William, was the first to leave England; my grandfather was the second. The first went to Australia to mine, the second to America. One daughter lived in Australia with her husband, and another daughter and their mother followed them to Australia, while five children remained in Cornwall. Like all risk-takers, the stories of these immigrants sound romantic and exciting. And yet there is something poignant about dying in a foreign country without all of one's family nearby. Only the daughter who lived in Perth attended her mother's burial. It's also sad to me that after thirty-three years of marriage, William and Elizabeth Jane's graves are half-way around the world from each other. I never met any of their eight children, including their second child, my grandfather, even though two of my great aunts, Lilly and Ada, were still alive when I was a small child. I wonder if my father was ever informed of his grandparents' deaths. I wish I'd had this information while he was alive. I think he would have loved looking at the family tree, and maybe he would have recognized the name Pentecost, and smiled.

WILLIAM TIPPETT AND SARAH ROGERS

I continued to work my way further up the family tree to find out who William Tippett's parents were, which meant searching for records going back to the late eighteenth century. I was not optimistic.

The first challenge was finding some kind of record of birth for my paternal great-great-grandfather, whose name I knew: William Tippett. And I could not find a baptism record either. I was reasonably sure he was born in 1796, thanks to the 1841 Census, in the county of Cornwall, England. I could speculate that he spent his entire adult life in Redruth, making it easy to assume that, like most Cornishmen of the time, he was born, lived and died in the same town.

William was a teenager in 1812 when the harvest failed in Cornwall. Because the price of wheat was too high for most mining families, barley was a staple of their diet. That year, angry miners in Redruth, who suspected the farmers were hoarding grain in order to keep the price inflated, marched to the houses of several farmers and forced them to sign an agreement to sell them wheat at a reasonable price. They also raided the

Redruth Brewery to get access to its stockpiles of barley. Talk about insurrection!

Most Cornish miners, in addition to their work underground, also farmed small lots on rented land, giving them another means of support, and it is likely William's family did the same. An excerpt from The West Briton newspaper dated July 1817 draws an excellent picture of life in Cornwall for a typical miner-farmer:

"Peter Skewes, a miner at Wheal Unity ("wheal" translates to "mine" in Cornish), resides at Blackwater in the parish of St. Agnes. He holds a small tenement consisting of about an acre and three-quarters of land, the soil of which is naturally sterile. This is divided into two nearly equal plots. One of these he plants with potatoes, the other he tills to wheat, and so on alternately, every year one of his little fields producing potatoes and the other wheat. By proper attention in the cultivation, he has on average eighty Cornish bushels of potatoes, and nine of wheat, each season. He keeps two donkeys, which graze on the straw of his wheat in the winter. With these he carries coals for his neighbors and collects manure for his ground. The refuse potatoes enable him to feed a pig, which, with fish purchased in the season, affords all that is required for food in addition to the produce of his fields and little garden. In this way has Peter Skewes passed the last seven years and supported a wife and family, now consisting of six children, not only without parish aid, but with a degree of comfort and independence of which there are not many examples in his situation in life."

The lifestyle described above is hardly one of wealth and ease. Although miner Peter Skewes avoided living on the dole, supported by the parish church, it was a hardscrabble life of living hand to mouth. A twenty-first-century American would see his life as pitiful, but in nineteenth-century rural Cornwall, it may have appeared not as dire.

During William's early life, emigration to America (and other countries) was becoming a fairly common occurrence. The local newspaper reported in spring 1818 that a ship had left Charlestown on the south coast of Cornwall with some fifty persons aboard, including entire families and a few older women who were joining their husbands who had emigrated months before "in pursuit of better fortune on a distant shore."

On September 11, 1823, when he was twenty-seven-years-old, William married Sarah Rogers, the thirty-two-year-old daughter of Benjamin and Elizabeth Knight Rogers from the St. Agnes parish near Redruth. They were married in St. Euny Church, the parish church of Redruth. Neither the bride nor the groom was literate, so the marriage record was signed by their X marks in the presence of two witnesses.

When England passed a law requiring the enumeration of its subjects every ten years, it was a blessing for genealogists everywhere and for

St. Euny Church, the parish church of Redruth in Cornwall."

all time. When information about an ancestor is scant at best, the Census provides at least minimal facts about who is in the family, when they were born and where, and where they were living that year. The first British census, taken in 1841, recorded that William and Sarah were living in Forge in Redruth with five children: four girls and an eight-year-old son also named William (who would become my great-grandfather). Sarah was pregnant with Helen, who was born later that year. Also in the household was William's youngest brother, Thomas, age twenty-five. William, the forty-year-old head of the household, was a copper miner, and although the census does not designate an occupation for Thomas, it is likely he too worked in the mines. It was customary for brothers to work together in the same mine, so it's possible that William and Thomas worked side by side every day. There are no records remaining to indicate which mine William and Thomas worked in, and it was common for miners to move around and work for whoever was hiring.

However, the conditions were the same in every Cornish mine: miserable. Descending the mine shaft, often 2,000 feet down, on a series of nearly vertical ladders, to his assigned gallery or level, the miner spent his day more than a quarter mile below the surface. Many mines tunneled far out under the sea, and it was not unusual for miners to actually feel the vibrations of the ocean above them. The spaces below were low, narrow chambers with rough rock walls that jutted out in all directions, often causing the unwary miner to injure himself before he even started to reach for his tools. The air that far underground was damp, hot and dusty, and thick with the acrid smell of gunpowder that was used for blasting the rock. His clothes would have been coated with red dust from the iron ore that was mixed in with the tin ore. Using a hammer and pick, the miner spent eight hours a day chiseling away at the hard rock, his work illuminated by the light of wax candles stuck to the rock walls by a handful of wet clay, a single candle affixed to his cloth hat. This was before matches were invented, and miners used flint, steel and tinder to produce a spark for lighting candles and igniting the explosives.

We don't know how far from the family home William and Thomas traveled to reach their place of employment. Most Cornish miners walked, often three or four miles, in every kind of weather, to the main mine shaft, changed their clothes in the drying house (called "the dry") and donned their underground work clothes to toil in temperatures reaching 100 degrees, only to emerge "to grass" eight hours later into pelting rain and biting winds and walk in darkness back to their cottages.

The family ate dinner together and the meal was typically salted fish, potatoes and tea. Because tea was quite expensive, dried mugwort leaves were often substituted. Many families kept a pig and when times were good, families could afford to buy pork from each other, serving it like home-cured bacon. Beef and mutton were rarely eaten by the working class. Due to the high price of wheat, Cornish mining families cooked with barley. Barley gruel was the usual breakfast, and barley bread was used by the women to make pasties, or hand pies, for the miner's lunch. Many Cornish families gathered samphire from the rocky cliffs. Samphire, also known as Herbe de St. Pierre, is a cliff plant with salty, fleshy leaves that housewives pickled and served with fish or seafood.

The cottages the miners built varied greatly according to the earnings of the family. Except in districts where loose stone suitable for building was plentiful, the miner generally built the walls of his house with cob, a mixture of clay and chopped straw that dried to the consistency of concrete. Many had up to six rooms, the upper one being under the high-pitched roof. The older cottages, however, were usually thatched and contained only two rooms, making for very crowded quarters for families that typically had several children. The floors were generally made of lime ash and tended to stay damp. Almost all had a garden plot where vegetables and potatoes were cultivated. Few if any of the cottages at this time had privies or possessed any system of drainage. There was no space in the older and smaller cottages to wash clothes indoors and hot water systems were totally unknown. Instead, water from the mines was used for doing the laundry, and large groups of women could be seen standing in the engine house washing the linen of their families in the warm water from the steam engine.

The Tippett family was living in the same cottage on the St. Agnes Road ten years later in 1851. Only three of their children were still at home. Twenty-four-year-old Emma worked as a dressmaker, their son William, then twenty, had joined his father working in the copper mines, and Helen, the youngest at eleven, was in school.

By the time of the 1861 Census, William had reached the age of sixty-four and Sarah was seventy years old. They were still living in Forge. William was farming six acres and had employed one boy to help him. Four grandchildren were living with them, the children of their daughter Jane Reynolds.

William died on March 22, 1869, in the village of Vose Vrose in Redruth. He was seventy-three. The informant on the death certificate was his son-in-law William Reynolds of Redruth, whose four children had been living in William's household eight years before. The cause of William's death was described as "natural decay."

William's widow, Sarah, was in her late seventies when he died. She was nearly blind and continued to live in the cottage in Forge with her granddaughter Elizabeth Reynolds, who was then a teenager. Sarah died seven years later on April 11, 1876, at the age of eighty-seven. Her son William, my great-grandfather, who could not read or write, signed the death record with his X mark, giving the cause of death as "old age."

Both William and Sarah lived unusually long lives. A miner who lived to seventy-three years of age was considered a remarkable feat given the dangerous and deplorable conditions in which he worked for almost fifty years. He did not die of the usual lung ailments that claimed the lives of most Cornish miners, like bronchitis or consumption (now known as tuberculosis). He did hard manual labor for all his life and in the end "natural decay" claimed him. Sarah bested his lifespan by fifteen years, and while she may have been infirm in her later years, to approach ninety in that day and age was quite impressive.

I had now traced my Tippett and Williams lines back four generations on my father's side. When added to four generations on my mother's side, my family tree was no longer looking like a blank slate. It had taken years of on-again-off-again work, several field trips to libraries and historical societies, one overseas pilgrimage to England, uncounted emails and phone calls. Today, my family tree has extended back several more generations, some branches all the way back to the early 1600s. But it was more fun for me to focus on the closest generations to me because that's where the stories can be best written. That's where wonderful old photos can be discovered, and where even an in-person, "I was there" interview is possible.

It occurred to me that maybe it was time to share some of these stories.

What's in a Name?

From an early age, I was reminded that I was named after my maternal great-grandmother Mary Ann Merrill. It wasn't until I got into genealogy as an adult that I could verify that my middle name, Lee, came from my father's mother, Corinda Lee Morrish. Tippett, of course, was my surname from birth.

When I got divorced in 1993, one of the thousands of issues that needed to be settled for the court was the last name of the divorcing woman. I knew I did not wish to keep my married name, but I also had to admit I didn't want to return to my maiden name either. I needed a fresh start. I was determined to re-define myself.

By that time, I'd done enough family history research that I had a nice collection of family surnames to consider for myself. Raplee? I didn't feel much connection with this family from upstate New York. Wagoner? I'd run into too many dead ends with this group and frankly didn't totally trust all the entries I'd made on my family tree. Hall? Maybe. Randall? This long line of colonial settlers was a real contender. Stoffer? There were so many different ways this name had been spelled in the past that I didn't want to take on more battles with how to spell my name than I already had. Anderton? Possibly. Speakman? That was my mother's maiden name, so that was out of the question. Ley? How was it pronounced: lay or lee? Too much confusion. Morrish? Merrill Morrish sounded like a character in a novel. Pentecost? My brother would have a fit. Williams? Hmmm. That sounded more melodious than the others, and was a tribute to my paternal great-grandmother, Catherine Lydia Williams.

I practiced saying "Merrill Lee Williams" over and over again until I was comfortable with it and it started to roll off my tongue. Granted, my new last name only added to the surfeit of double letters, and I had to practice writing my full name out until I could develop a certain flourish to my signature. My sons were a bit confused and wondered where I'd come up with that idea. "Williams? Who's *that?*" asked my son Eric. "Nobody I know in our family is named Williams!"

My younger son, Doug, had the advantage of being apprised of my decision earlier than Eric, who felt like a bomb had dropped on his head. Doug knew for a while that I had been considering different names and understood my need for change. He applauded my unorthodox decision but warned me about how my own mother might react. "Nana probably won't say anything out loud," he said, "but she will still disapprove. She's very good at letting her opinions be known without saying a word." He was right: My mother was silent, her signal that she wasn't happy.

My friends, who had no knowledge of my family tree, were confused and frustrated. With time, however, most mustered a show of support by remembering to use my new last name. There were a few holdouts who enjoyed poking me by deliberately calling me by my married name, but I've learned to smile and change the subject.

By now, more than twenty-five years later, everyone around me knows me as Merrill Williams, and is comfortable saying it. And I'm comfortable with it too. But it was always more than just getting used to new sounds. When I look over my family tree, I belong there in more ways than just birth order. I am inextricably part of the whole. Merrill Lee Williams was a perfectly natural choice, after all.

Who Cares About Ancestors?

When my mother turned eighty, our family staged a small family reunion at my home in Ojai, California. Mom's brother, Jack Speakman, arrived from Kansas City, and there was a very touching scene on my back patio as these two siblings greeted each other after so many years. They were both pretty frail, a bit unsteady on their feet, and more than a little bedazzled by all the fuss we were making.

I was anxious to talk to my Uncle Jack and tell him I had embarked on building a family tree. Sitting alone with him later that day, I asked if I could pose a few questions about the Speakman family. He looked somewhat bewildered, shrugged his shoulders and replied, "Well, I guess so." I started off carefully, asking about his parents, my grandparents, who had passed away long ago. Shaking his head, Uncle Jack looked at me with a smile and said, "Who cares? They're all dead and there's not much I can tell you about them." I was stunned, and also a little offended. Who cares? Well, I do. How, I wondered, could he dismiss our ancestors so easily? There isn't a malicious bone in my uncle's body, but I suddenly felt compelled to protect our ancestors from being forgotten, brushed away like so many crumbs on the table.

I looked around at the people who had gathered in my back yard to celebrate a birthday, to celebrate family. How could they fully understand their family if they didn't know the stories of their parents, their grandparents, their great-grandparents? I didn't argue then with Uncle Jack, but I certainly didn't agree with him. I was sure he wanted his own children to know his life story, as I also want mine to know about me and their grandparents. I don't want my children to go through life thinking that the world begins and ends with them. I want them to understand that they are truly a natural outcome of all those who preceded them. I, for one, am an American because I have a grandfather and a great-grandfather who decided to leave England and settle in America. I have a college degree because my parents valued education and worked hard to pay for it. I was taught by them to love my family.

I thought about the generations that preceded us, and all the things that had to go right for me to be here today. These were the people who survived illness and disease, who did not lose their lives in a war, who were healthy enough to produce children who in turn lived to keep the family line going.

I looked over at my mother who had chosen to celebrate her eightieth birthday by getting a laser peel on her face. Although the procedure had taken place a month before, her face was still taut, shiny and red. It looked painful. All the photos of her from that weekend made her face bright purple. She looked like a beet. Weeks later, when assembling a commemorative album, I would end up throwing out all those terrible photos that made a mockery of my beautiful mother. I realized as I was discarding those snapshots that I was editing a chapter in her life. Is that acceptable behavior for a family historian? Perhaps not, but I did it more as a protective measure. I did it to ensure that the younger generation would know her as she was in the best of times, the person as she really looked, not transmogrified by a medical procedure that did her more harm than good.

I realized in that moment that however I chose to proceed with my family research, the end result, this book, would be up to me. Indeed, a fair amount of editing was done all along the way. Some stories I found more interesting than others. Some of my book's characters were more endearing to me than others. Being female, the plight of the women in my family was more meaningful to me than that of some of the men whose achievements were undeniably impressive. While always attempting to stay as close to the truth as I could, their stories have been filtered through my eyes and heart.

As a regular viewer of the television series "Finding Your Roots," I am constantly struck by how emotional most guests get when presented with their family's history. Some shed tears. Most are stunned by the huge constellation of names on their expanded family trees. Reactions vary from "I have all these people to thank" to "I realize now that I am a small part in the long flow of humanity" to "These are my people. Now I know who I am." For me, every discovery I made while building my family tree was emotional. Those old photos touched me more than I thought possible. Even finding a digitized image of an ancestor's signature was moving for me.

I often fantasize about meeting my ancestors in person. That somehow, through the miracle of time travel, I could approach one of them, introduce myself and tell them how I found them after all these years. I would assure them that their lives are still influencing their descendants, that indeed they live on within us. I would want to gaze into their eyes and find physical resemblances between us, touch their clothing, listen to their voices and hear the cadences of their English accents. How would they greet me? With bemusement, probably. Astonished at my clothing and hair style, casual comportment, and bewildered at my American accent. But in the end, I imagine, we would all cherish knowing each other, and celebrate.

Who cares about my ancestors? I do. Deeply.

Acknowledgements

Every book, even small ones like this, requires the participation of many people. No author writes alone. I am grateful beyond measure to those who helped me along the way:

My sister-in-law, Erika Tippett, who shares the genealogy gene with me and was my side-by-side companion in our research into the Tippett ancestors, and a fact-checker par excellence.

Kelly Speakman Webb, who blessed me with numerous clarifications on our shared grandparents, and patiently took me on a driving tour of the homes of our relatives in Kansas City.

Glen Caldwell Speakman, my half-uncle, who shared many stories about the man who was his father and my grandfather.

The volunteers at the Doris Foley Historical Research Library in Nevada City, California who found many critical documents on my great-grandparents William and Catherine Morrish, my ancestors who left Cornwall and settled in Grass Valley to work in the mines and sell produce from their famous garden.

Jim Collins, volunteer, LaSalle County Genealogy Guild, Ottawa, Illinois, who cheerfully contributed research on my Speakman, Stofer, Randall and Gee ancestors who left England, then upstate New York to farm the plains of Illinois.

Jean Staunton, Assistant Library Coordinator, Cornish Association of Victoria, who helped me track down my great uncle William John Tippett who left Cornwall in 1884 for the goldfields of Australia.

Katrina and Fred Frape, my dear British friends who spend half the year in Ojai, California, and the rest of the year in England. They were my companions on my trip to Cornwall, providing their home, their car, their expertise and great sense of humor. Their generosity and hospitality will never be forgotten.

MERRILL WILLIAMS FAMILY TREE

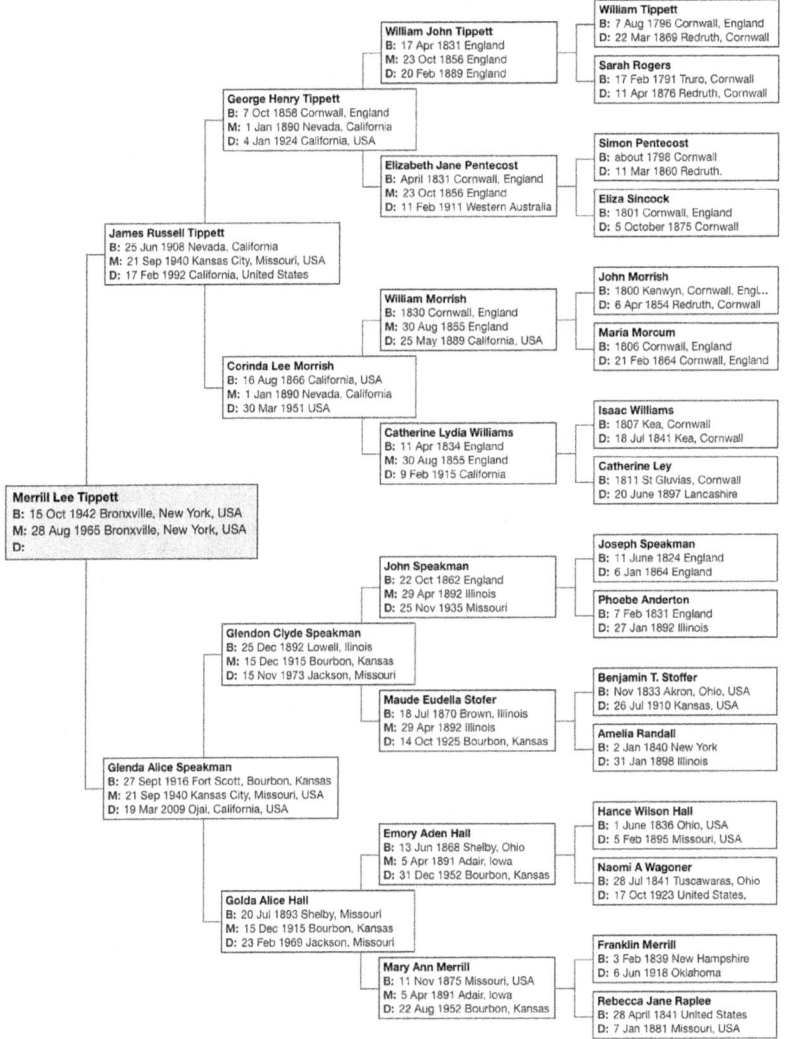

Map of Cornwall

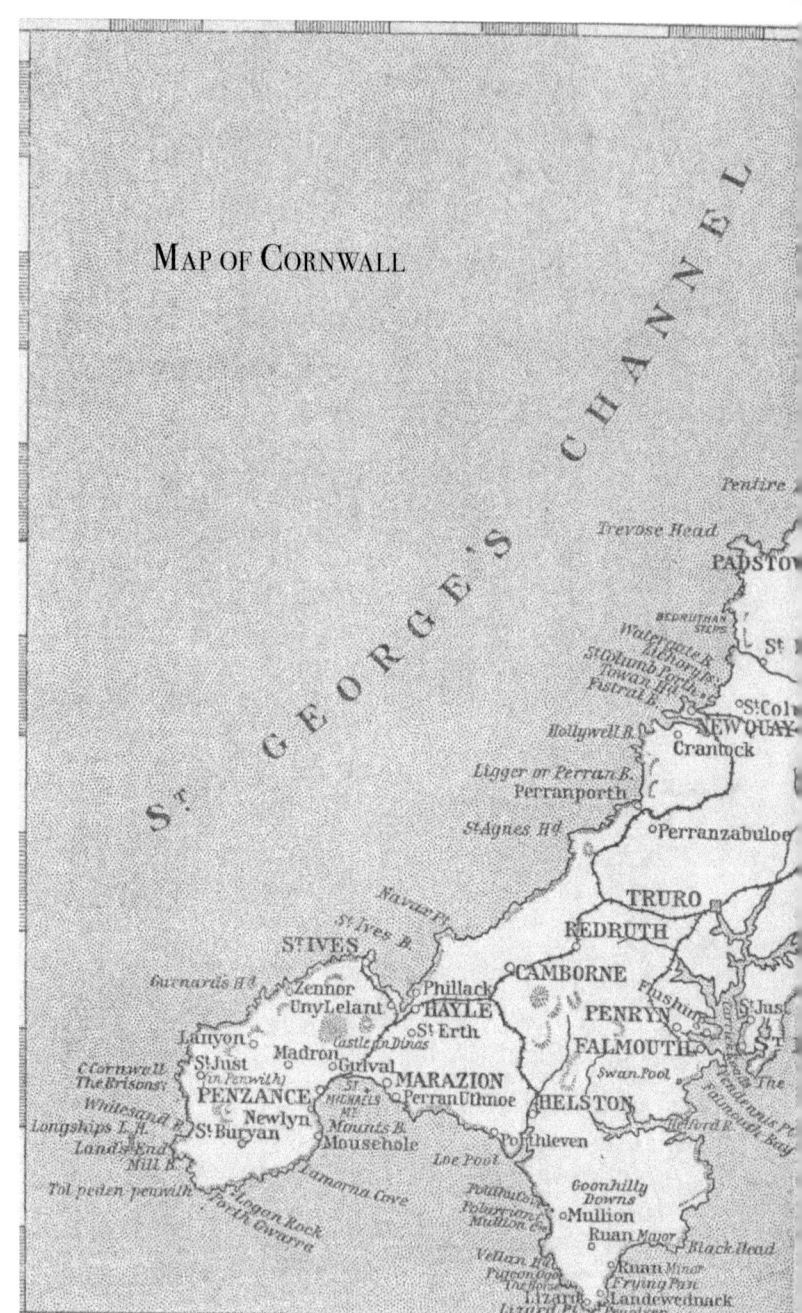